Christine A. Yared

PRIVATE LOVE, PUBLIC SCHOOL – GAY TEACHER UNDER FIRE

Christine A. Yared is an attorney, writer, educator, and activist. For over thirty years Christine's work has centered on LGBTQ+ legal, political, and social issues. Christine has taught about and fought against discrimination based on LGBTQ+ identity, gender, race, ethnicity, and against sexual harassment. Her cases and advocacy have been covered by numerous media outlets. She resides in Grand Rapids, Michigan.

Are you a teacher with a story to share? Would you like to have Christine speak to your book club or organization?

- Contact Christine at christine@christineyared.com

Connect with Christine

- Sign-up for her newsletter at www.christineyared.com

and follow her on:

- Facebook   www.facebook.com/gayteacher
- Twitter   @christineyared
- Instagram   www.instagram.com/cayared

Private Love, Public School

Gay Teacher Under Fire

Private Love, Public School

Gay Teacher Under Fire

Christine A. Yared

PENNING HISTORY PRESS, LLC
GRAND RAPIDS, MICHIGAN

Private Love, Public School – Gay Teacher Under Fire

Copyright © 2021 by Christine A. Yared

ISBN 978-1-7352371-0-7 (Paperback)
ISBN 978-1-7352371-1-4 (eBook)

LCCN 2020921773

Book cover by Damonza
Book interior design and layout by Clark Kenyon
Book cover author photograph by Michelle Burroughs

Printed in the United States of America

Penning History Press, LLC
Grand Rapids, Michigan

www.christineyared.com
christine@christineyared.com

Photo credits:(1) Olan Mills, Inc.; photograph courtesy of Randy Block. (2) and (3) Taken by author. (4) T. J. Hamilton, *The Grand Rapids Press* / Grand Rapids Public Museum. (5) and (6) Lori Niedenfuer Cool / *The Grand Rapids Press*, Grand Rapids Public Museum. (7) Mary Banghart Therrien / The Lesbian and Gay Community Network.

With love to my daughter,
Leigh Alexandria Yared

The critical impulse we need to develop involves a commitment to use knowledge in a transformative way. To use knowledge to help remake the world so that it is better for all of its inhabitants. This critical impulse means that we have to absolutely refuse to attribute any kind of permanency to that which is, simply because it is.

Angela Davis
October 10, 2006
"How Does Change Happen?"
University of California, Davis

medium.com/@angelicacoleman/
how-does-change-happen-906eaf9bd9b5

Contents

Foreword

I first became aware of Gerry Crane and the struggles he endured as a teacher in the Byron Center Public Schools after he was outed, back in 1996 when I read an article in *Between the Lines*, Michigan's LGBTQ newspaper. When one looks back at that period in time, it's amazing to consider the progress that has been made on LGBTQ rights over the past two decades. In 1996 same-sex couples could not marry nor have their relationship recognized by the State of Michigan or the federal government. Laws criminalizing private, same-sex sodomy between consenting adults were constitutional and could be used to justify discrimination against LGBTQ people, since they were presumed to engage in illegal sexual behaviors. Only a handful of Michigan cities and townships had local ordinances protecting LGBTQ people from discrimination. Neither Michigan nor federal civil rights laws provided explicit protections against discrimination on the basis of sexual orientation or gender identity.

Today same-sex sodomy laws are unconstitutional. Same-sex couples can marry and receive the federal and state recognition and the benefits afforded by marriage. Close to four dozen Michigan cities and ordinances prohibit discrimination against LGBT people. And yet still today, neither Michigan nor federal civil rights laws provide explicit protections against discrimination on the basis of sexual orientation and gender identity.

Which brings me to Aimee Stephens, a transgender woman, whom the ACLU represented in her employment discrimination claim before the United States Supreme Court and whose case was part of the 2020 landmark decision in *Bostock v. Clayton County*, which held that LGBT people are protected against employment discrimination under Title VII, a federal civil rights law that prohibits discrimination on the basis of sex. In other words, discrimination against an employee for being gay or lesbian or transgender is sex discrimination. If only this decision had been issued at the time Gerry Crane experienced his discrimination by the Byron Center school district and community.

I was both honored and fortunate to work with and get to know closely Aimee Stephens during the course of her litigation. Like Gerry Crane, she was both deeply passionate about and committed to her job. As an embalmer for the Harris Funeral Homes, Aimee believed that she had both a mission and a purpose to help families in their most vulnerable time of grief. She wanted to ensure that they would see their loved ones in the way that they most remembered them. Like Gerry Crane, Aimee's work was highly valued by both the funeral home and the families she worked with. Also like Gerry Crane, Aimee struggled for years with her ability to be her authentic self in the workplace. When she finally summoned the courage to come out to her employer, she was summarily fired from her job.

Often when we look at seminal LGBT civil rights cases, we regard the plaintiffs in the abstract. We don't consider the full extent of harm that these people have suffered due to the discrimination. For Aimee, it was not only the indignity of being fired for being transgender, but also the loss of income which created financial stresses for herself and family. It was the loss of her sense of purpose, which triggered depression, and in my opinion, a downward spiral in her health. And yet Aimee decided that she wasn't going to accept this kind of treatment by her former employer and that she was going to do something about it. She wanted to make sure that other transgender people did not suffer the same fate as she did. Although somewhat shy and reticent, Aimee embraced her role as spokesperson for her case, sharing her personal story and why she felt that the way she was treated was wrong. Despite suffering from kidney failure and respiratory issues, Aimee was determined that she would help others through her case. And through this process, Aimee found her new purpose in life and felt a tremendous responsibility to her transgender community.

I was with Aimee in Washington, DC, when her case was heard before the United States Supreme Court. The day before the hearing, Aimee did back-to-back interviews with the media, one after another, from morning until later afternoon, until she collapsed from physical exhaustion. She attended the hearing the next morning in a wheel chair. After the hearing, as she was wheeled out to the front of the Supreme Court building, she was greeted by a roar of cheers and applause, and chants of "We Love You" and "Thank You" from the crowds who had gathered in support. I stood by Aimee with her wife, Donna, and watched as countless young people, many who were transgender, came up to her thanking her for her courage to tell her story and to stand up for her and their rights. Later, Aimee said that was the most memorable experience of her involvement with this case.

When she came back home and as her health further declined, Aimee maintained her commitment to the cause of transgender rights, joining the Board of SAGE Metro Detroit, an organization that focuses on LGBT older adults, serving as ambassador to the transgender older adult community. While awaiting the Supreme Court decision, Aimee continued to hope that she would live long enough to read the Supreme Court's opinion. Unfortunately, that was not to meant to be, as Aimee passed away on May 12, 2020, more than a month before the historic decision in her case and at the far-too-young age of fifty-nine. The Supreme Court decision is Aimee's legacy and she fulfilled her second life purpose—making a positive difference in the lives of transgender people.

Like Aimee, Gerry's story is an important one that needs to be told. LGBT discrimination existed in 1996 and still exists today.

Both Aimee and Gerry had much to offer to this world and were treated unfairly for living their authentic lives. We need to pass both Michigan and federal civil rights laws that explicitly mention sexual orientation and gender identity and make it clear that LGBT people are to be accorded the same dignity in all aspects of life. The harm and the collateral damage caused by LGBT discrimination is real.

Jay Kaplan
Attorney
ACLU of Michigan
Nancy Katz and Margo Dichtemiller LGBT Rights Project

Author's Note

This is a nonfiction work. All people named in the book are actual individuals. In a few instances, names have been changed for privacy purposes. The material in this book is based on interviews, documents, articles, oral histories, other papers, and where applicable, my recollection of events.

In writing the book I have been sensitive to the fact that Gerry's students were teenagers. They were in a life stage where they were exploring their own identity and views while still being under the strong influence of their parents, extended family, clergy, and school officials. Many students came to Gerry privately, often in tears, upset about being required by their parents to drop his class and about others things that were happening. Some were pressured by adults in their lives to do and say things that they otherwise would not have done. Nothing in this book is meant to criticize, deride, or blame any of the students for outcomes beyond their control.

⁓

While I have been writing throughout my career as an attorney, professor, and activist, this is my first book. I intended to write what I billed as a traditional nonfiction book. But it was not that simple.

After learning about the narrative nonfiction genre, I started to experiment with that approach. I came to realize that on some level I needed to insert myself more directly into this book.

I was already in the book, though shrouded. Gerry and I came of age, and came out, in similar political times. We shared a common geographic terrain in west Michigan. We also came to briefly know each other because of the controversy. I have introduced myself into the narrative where needed to write the book that I needed to write, using methods that best reflect my voice.

I hope that you will be moved by and will in some way learn from Gerry's story.

Acknowledgments

I am grateful to everyone who agreed to be interviewed for my book. Thank you to those who were exceptionally generous with their time and patient with my numerous requests. These contributions were invaluable to me. I appreciate those who spoke with me even though it was difficult emotionally or risky because they were concerned that their contribution might affect their employment. Many thanks also to those who responded when I reached out for specific information or input.

I am especially grateful to Randy Block for graciously sharing stories and recollections, and making material available for my research. I am grateful to the work of the late Dr. Paul Kutsche, founder of the Kutsche Office of Local History at Grand Valley State University, who conducted interviews and gathered documents related to Gerry Crane's ordeal, all of which were invaluable for my research. Many thanks to Julie Tabberer and everyone else with the Grand Rapids History & Special Collections at the Grand Rapids Public Library who helped with my use of the Grand Rapids Lesbian and Gay Organizations Project Collection, and to Alex Forist, Chief Curator for the Grand Rapids Public Museum.

I am privileged to live in a time in human history and in a place in the world where I have been able to choose to live my personal and professional life openly as a lesbian. I recognize the plight of those who, like Gerry Crane, have suffered greatly and those who continue to experience pain or risk death for being out or after being outed. I am grateful to the generations of LGBTQ+ people, some of whom inhabit recorded history, but most of whom are lost to the ages, who in large or small ways lived out of the closet before the coining of that phrase and who, because of their courage, endured devastating consequences. My strength, and the strength of the LGBTQ+ movement, is borne in part, through their pain.

I am tremendously grateful to the people who contributed to my Kickstarter campaign: William R. Baldridge, Ruth McNally Barshaw, Donna Chaney, Anne Dill, Dr. Slawomir Dobrzanski, Carol Dodge, Jeff Grim, Dr. Will Hall, Jacob [last name anonymous], Nidal Kanaan, Claudia Kerbawy, Marilyn Klar, Sean Kosofsky, Dr. Michelle Lee, Anita Levin, Jessica Kerbawy Niven, Dennis B. Murphy, Fadi William Musleh, PFLAG Holland/Lakeshore, Tony Reese, Harvey Rowland, Fred Sebulske, Dr. Jill Van Antwerp, Marian Vanderwall, Franklin Blain Van Pelt, Glynn Warren, and Bill Young. You helped to provide me with the means to delve into the self-publishing process, and each contribution buoyed my spirit.

Thank you to everyone who has cheered me on over the years by offering me words of support, asking questions about the book, or commenting on or "liking" my Gay Teacher Facebook page and other social media. You have all helped to energize me throughout my writing process. Thank you also to Grand Rapids' area coffee-houses and bookstores which served as homes for my writing. They are a haven for those of us who engage in solitary work.

I owe special gratitude to the people in my nonfiction writing group, especially Debbie Aliya, Phil Van Huffel, and Joe Stankowski. Your ongoing input and camaraderie has been invaluable. You have helped me to liberate my writing from the constraints inherent in standard legal writing. I especially appreciate Debbie Aliya's persistent nudge for me to place myself in the story. You correctly asserted that it was necessary, that it would open my writing and help me find my voice.

Thank you to my college friend Ruth McNally Barshaw, cartoonist, writer, artist, and creator of *Ellie McDoodle*, for your enthusiastic support. Your creative spirit, persistence, and accomplishments have been a source of inspiration for me.

Thank you to Stephanie Hoover for bringing together a group of strong, accomplished women writers by founding the Vixens of Nonfiction. I greatly appreciate and have benefited from this group, especially those who have been a part of our Vixens online meetings during the past several months.

I am indebted to Dr. Kathleen Blumreich for her invaluable insights, suggestions, and edits after reading my manuscript. I deeply appreciate everyone who read an earlier draft of the book, or portions of it, and who shared their input and suggestions— Debbie Aliya, Dr. Karen Chaney, Michelle Crooks, Anne Dill, Mary Juhlin, Dr. Michelle Lee, Megan Morrissey, Sue Perry, Maris Stella "Star" Swift, Leigh Yared, and Abby Young.

I am grateful to Anne Dill for her valuable input, ongoing support and encouragement. Special thanks to Abby Young for her exceptional work as sound engineer for the audiobook. Many thanks to my legal assistant, Dawn Draper; author assistant, Jennifer Butcher; and my former Grand Valley State University student and intern, Brody Cragg, all who provided critical services at various junctures during my research and writing of this book. Thank you also to Oliver Yared for his critical technological assistance.

Special thanks to Rivka Hodgkinson for creating a top-notch author website and for her valuable insights about technology and social media. Thank you to Damonza for designing an exceptional book cover, to Clark Kenyon for creating a professional interior book design and layout, to Kristin Chaney Hagan for her creative input, to Michelle Burroughs for her photography, and to indexer Meridith Murray.

I am greatly indebted to my editor, Susan Matheson, for her patience, steadfast support, and exceptional work. From our first meeting, she understood the critical need for Gerry's story to be documented, and she maintained her commitment to the book even though the project took longer than expected. She greatly elevated the quality of the book.

I am grateful to Jay Kaplan, attorney with the ACLU of Michigan, for writing a thoughtful and timely foreword for my book. Over the years Jay has been at the forefront of important developments in LGBTQ+ equality, including representing Aimee Stephens in the landmark 2020 case banning LGBTQ+-based employment discrimination. I have worked with and enjoyed the benefit of Jay's skill and insights on numerous cases over the years, and I appreciate his willingness to contribute to this book.

I especially thank and express my deep love to the children of my life—Richard Kyle Palmitier, Abby Young, Molly Young Hoxha, and Leigh Alexandria Yared. You have all enriched and brought great joy to my life. I am grateful for the life of and love from my daughter, Leigh Alexandria Yared. You have been my consistent supporter and inspiration throughout the years and years of starts and stops on this book.

I am tremendously thankful for my wife, Dr. Karen A. Chaney, for her unwavering support, encouragement, and wisdom and for the hours she spent reading, editing, and discussing the substantive and publishing aspects of the book with me. Her insights and expertise about religious history and theology were especially invaluable to me. Karen, I am grateful for and treasure our life together.

Introduction

In 1993, when Gerry Crane was twenty-nine years old, he began working as a high school music teacher in Byron Center, a small, conservative suburb of Grand Rapids, Michigan. In the summer of 1995, before same-sex marriage was legal, Gerry and his partner, Randy Block, decided they wanted to exchange vows in a commitment ceremony, which would take place in the fall. Despite their best efforts to keep their ceremony private, students, parents, and school administrators of Byron Center High School found out, and many people in this religiously and politically conservative town were upset. However no one could have predicted the extent of the fallout and how Gerry's life would turn upside down.

I first met Gerry and Randy during the public controversy that erupted after their ceremony. At that time, I served on the board of directors of The Lesbian, Gay and Bisexual Community Network of West Michigan (The Network), worked as an attorney specializing in LGBTQ+ law, and taught law courses at Grand Valley State University.[1, 2] I am gay and at the time was raising young children with my partner. Gerry's situation spoke to my identity, my family, my work, my activism, and my core values.

I set out to write this book because of Gerry. I felt strongly that his experience needed to be documented, told, and remembered. And in the spirit of his devotion to teaching, I sought lessons to be learned from his experience at Byron Center High School. While this controversy most affected Gerry, it also became a transformative experience for others in his life—his partner, friends, students, and fellow church members. I also wrote this book for those students and teachers who are trying to make sense of what happened to them in the past and those who are struggling now.

This is my attempt to help create change for students and teachers in the future.

Cultural and Legal Landscape

Gerry and Randy's commitment ceremony took place in October 1995. At that time LGBTQ+ people were largely deemed unacceptable in society and were condemned as "deviants." The majority culture did not support what was inaccurately referred to as "the homosexual lifestyle."

In 1986, the US Supreme Court upheld a Georgia law that criminalized sodomy between consenting adults. The court ruled that Georgia's criminal law was constitutional even as applied to the defendant, Michael Hardwick, who had engaged in sex with another man in the privacy of his bedroom.[3] This case was not overturned until 2003.[4]

During the Byron Center controversy, marriage equality was a charged political issue. In June 1995, Michigan Governor John Engler signed a law banning same-sex marriage and prohibiting the recognition of out-of-state same-sex marriage. Congress followed suit, and in 1996 President Bill Clinton signed into law the anti-gay Defense of Marriage Act (DOMA), which was based on the notion that same-sex marriage was an assault on heterosexual marriage. DOMA defined marriage as being between one man and one woman and excluded gay couples from federal benefits available to heterosexual couples. The law also gave states the right to not recognize the rights of same-sex couples married in another state.

The Supreme Court did not rule DOMA unconstitutional until 2013.[5] Two years later, the Court legalized same-sex marriage.[6] In June 2020, the Supreme Court ruled that employers cannot discriminate against people based on their sexual orientation or gender identity.[7]

It might appear that these groundbreaking cases occurred at

warp speed. That is not the case. The rulings reflect generations of grassroots action. The most powerful driving force that led to these recent Supreme Court decisions has been LGBTQ+ people throughout the country coming out—to their friends, family, co-workers, service providers, and spiritual communities—one person at a time. In most cases this was painful; in many cases it was devastating. Eventually, however, fewer straight people were saying that they did not know anyone who was gay or lesbian. As more people came out in the various aspects of their lives, many straight people began to question and confront their own homophobia, although others continue to justify or deny it. In this way the LGBTQ+ civil rights movement is the embodiment of grassroots action.

Gerry and Randy contributed to this process. They held a commitment ceremony at a time when doing so carried risk. Once outed, Gerry did not run away or hide. He held his head high and moved through the pain.

Despite the landmark court cases, people who identify as LGBTQ+ continue to be subjected to discrimination and hate crimes. Homophobia and transphobia permeate numerous aspects of their lives.[8] Many LGBTQ+ teachers, in particular, face discrimination, live closeted lives, and work in fear of losing their employment. At the same time, an increasing number of students are struggling with their sexual orientation and gender identity at earlier ages. They face bullying, rejection, physical violence, and sometimes death by suicide.

Gerry's story sheds light on crucial questions that are relevant today—the application of the First Amendment, including the separation of church and state, and the scope of equal protection as applied to LGBTQ+-related issues in public schools. Gerry's story also explores his personal journey of reconciling being gay and Christian, as well as the debate within his church and his broader

Christian community. In doing so, this book focuses attention on practices and dialogues about homosexuality which are still happening today within some places of worship.

Gerry's story began in 1995, before most celebrities came out to the public and before popular television shows and movies featured LGBTQ+ characters. As a cultural marker, Ellen DeGeneres came out in 1997, and the television show *Will & Grace* did not begin until 1998. While reading this book, it is important to be cognizant of the cultural and legal context of that time.

Terminology and Stylistic Decisions

During the past several decades, the terms used to express a person's sexuality, gender expression, and gender identity have evolved. Current terminology is precise and reflects a more nuanced understanding of sexuality and gender. The term "gay" generally refers to a person whose enduring physical, romantic, and/or emotional attractions are to people of the same sex. The term "gay" includes lesbians and gay men. In an attempt to create a term which incorporates a variety of identities, the acronym LGBTQ+, which stands for lesbian, gay, bisexual, transgender, queer, and other identities, has been adopted and is more widely used today.

Those who oppose people who identify as LGBTQ+ often use the term "homosexual," especially in the context of discussing their anti-gay religious-based beliefs. By the late 1960s, the term "homosexual" went out of favor by those in the gay community. It was considered limiting and clinical, and the word "homo" has been used in a disparaging manner.

This book tells the story of the reactions to a teacher's sexual orientation in the mid-1990s before the adoption of the term "LGBTQ+" and addresses beliefs about religion and homosexuality. For these reasons, and for stylistic considerations, I use the word "homosexuality" in the context of religious beliefs, and at other times I use the term "gay." At the end of the book I use the term "LGBTQ+" which is consistent with the focus of the final two chapters. However, while Gerry was discriminated against based on his sexual orientation, not his gender identity, this narrative contains elements that are central to the stories of many LGBTQ+ people.

Gerry Crane often complained to his students about the color of his classroom. It was drab, and aesthetics mattered to Gerry. One day during spring break, Gerry went to school to do some work. As he walked down the hall, he heard a commotion coming from his classroom. He opened the door, and what he saw made him laugh—a group of students were painting his classroom.

Gerry's students valued what he brought to the classroom—a passion for music, the ability to motivate them to do their best, and humor. They wanted to surprise him by brightening the room where he taught.

This was the year before his commitment ceremony. It would be this mutual respect, his engagement with students, and his passion for his work that would carry Gerry through what was to come.

1

Signs

Gerry Crane is one of our best teachers on staff at Byron Center High School. He has raised the standard of both our vocal music and band programs. He has been a good role model for our students in how he conducts himself as a professional and [in] the high expectations he maintains for himself and his students.

William Skilling
Byron Center High School Principal
Gerry Crane's June 1995 Performance Evaluation

The doors to the high school gym were locked. Despite the crisp December weather and the frenzy of the approaching holidays, the hallway was packed with people waiting to get inside for the school board meeting. Over six hundred students, parents, clergy, reporters, and community members waited. Security guards were scattered throughout the area. Many people were clustered in small groups. Some clutched their Bibles. Several people held signs with Bible verses. Two women were quoting scriptures to each other, with one woman asking the other, "Why can't they change? It's sinful." Others sported "Welcome to Salem" buttons in orange and black, the colors of the high school.

It was December 18, 1995, and this board meeting was the fourth one in as many weeks. All meetings had focused on the future of the music teacher.[9] Gerry Crane had taught at the high school for three years, and during that brief time he had built a flourishing music department. By all accounts he was a talented musician and an asset to the school. He was in his element in the classroom. A natural teacher, Gerry held his students to high standards while using humor to keep them engaged. His students sensed that he cared about them. They opened up to him about their struggles. He nourished their self-esteem. What was the problem? The board had been informed that Gerry was gay and had recently formalized his relationship with Randy Block, his partner of three years, in a commitment ceremony.

Many constituents of Byron Center High School, a public school located in religiously and politically conservative west Michigan, believed that homosexuality was contrary to the law of God, that homosexuals were deviant and that as such, they should not be teaching their children.[10] Others thought that a teacher's sexual orientation was irrelevant.

All agreed, however, that Gerry's teaching abilities were not at issue; even those wanting him fired spoke well of him as a teacher. Parents who did not want their children to be taught by a gay person would preface their opinion with comments such as, "I give him credit for building the music program," or "There's no denying that he's a talented teacher."

Michigan and federal law did not prohibit discrimination against gay employees. In addition, Gerry's union contract did not prohibit discrimination based on sexual orientation. As a tenured teacher, Gerry could only be fired for "reasonable and just cause," for example, having a sexual relationship with a student or failing to show up for classes. Arguably his sexuality did not constitute a reasonable and just cause. Yet Michigan's tenure law had not addressed that question.

At issue were the religious values of the community. Rev. Richard Gregory, minister at Byron Center Bible Church, was the national executive director of the Independent Fundamentalist Churches of America. The high school principal, William Skilling, attended Rev. Gregory's church. The minister framed the issue as whether the Byron Center community would allow the homosexual "lifestyle" to be affirmed as normal. Rev. Gregory and most people in the school district demanded that their public school resolve this question based on fundamentalist religious beliefs.

Byron Center is a suburb located thirteen miles south of downtown Grand Rapids and about thirty miles east of Lake Michigan. In 1995, the population of Byron Center was approximately three thousand and the population of the greater Byron Center area, Byron Township, was approximately thirteen thousand. At the time there were 529 students at the high school, and drivers entering the city were greeted with the sign: "Welcome to Byron Center, a growing community with a small town style." More than 40 percent of the residents were of Dutch heritage and another 20 percent were of German descent. Most residents belonged to a Christian church, such as Byron Center Bible Church, First Christian Reformed Church, Byron Center United Methodist Church, or St. Sebastian's Catholic Church. Today, one-third of Byron Center parents send their children to local parochial schools.

"Many parents who send their children to Byron Center Public Schools believe their children are attending a Christian school," explained Jim Jauw, a parent who had had two sons in Gerry's classes. "People who move into the community are typically asked two questions: 'What do you do for a living?' and 'What church do you attend?'"

Gerry had been teaching at Byron Center since 1993. In July 1995, he obtained tenure at age thirty-one. Gerry, a good-looking man, had a medium frame, with brown hair, a neatly trimmed beard and mustache, and expressive eyes.

Years earlier, Gerry, a lifelong Christian, had considered entering the ministry but ultimately concluded that he was called to serve young people as a music teacher. He attended college in west Michigan and was well aware of the conservative Christian environment. In fact, Gerry's evangelical upbringing gave him a common cultural language and shared sensibility with devout Christians. He was comfortable being around people who centered their lives around their Christian beliefs. Most of his closest relationships were rooted in a shared Christian faith. Of course, Gerry understood that many people in Byron Center did not share his belief that God created gay people—that homosexuality was consistent with Christianity. For that reason, he had regularly taken precautions to keep his personal life private. He did not talk about Randy, or their life together, in the school setting. When Randy attended school musical performances, he drove separately to the school and only briefly interacted with Gerry after the event. Two months earlier, in October 1995, when the couple had committed their lives to each other, exchanging vows and rings in a private ceremony, Gerry did not openly share this news with his colleagues.

The school district's and community's reactions reflected their vehement anti-gay sentiment—views that originated in their religious belief that homosexuality was a grievous sin and that they were called to "hate the sin, love the sinner." There appeared to be an exception to the "love the sinner" rule: when a gay person taught your children. In the 1980s, during the Reagan era, the rise of the religious right's Moral Majority fueled anti-gay rhetoric in public schools. Founded in 1979 by Rev. Jerry Falwell, the Moral Majority's success was facilitated in great part by their strategy of identifying and encouraging people with shared views to run for office on their school boards.

Unknown to Gerry, a student whom Gerry had earlier disciplined found out about the ceremony from his family. The student went to the venue and surreptitiously obtained a program of the ceremony. Armed with this "evidence," and by implication evidence of Gerry's sexual orientation, the student's parent contacted the school to complain. In short order, word spread throughout the local community: their high school music teacher was gay and, in their view, he had *married* a man.[11]

Parents immediately pulled their students out of Gerry's classes, and many demanded that Gerry be dismissed. Local newspapers were filled with letters from community members expressing opposition to or support for Gerry Crane. The school received approximately four thousand letters about Gerry.[12] One man warned the school that if they did not fire Gerry, other gay teachers at the school would come out. A couple of people said that the school would need to worry about teachers with AIDS. A mother instructed Gerry to do the Christ-like act of resigning and leaving Byron Center in peace. Another warned that Satan's work was destroying the fabric of our society.

A mother of a student wrote, "Our music department has begun to flourish because of Mr. Crane's hard work and dedication. If you look deeper, you will find much more support for this man than there are people against him. His private life is just that." The woman identified herself as Christian, and ended her letter by asking, "There are too many prejudices in the world. Can't we help eliminate one?"[13]

Time dragged as the people who were crowded together in the school hallway waited for the gym doors to open. While a few people waiting identified as non-Christian, atheist, or agnostic, most of the people derived their core values from the way their Christian religion interpreted the Bible. Others asserted that religion was irrelevant: this was a public school governed by the constitutional separation between church and state.

For the gay people in attendance, including Christians, the sights and sounds of people using the Bible to justify firing a teacher for being gay cut to the core of their identity. It was painful to hear others make public pronouncements about the value of their life based on their sexuality. It was even more painful to know that there were gay students hearing these degrading statements at a time when the students were likely struggling to come to terms with their own sexuality.

Some gay people in the hallway were living closeted or partially closeted lives steeped in fear—fear of losing the love and companionship of their family and friends; fear of losing rights to and time with their children or losing the opportunity to even have children; fear of being subjected to emotional, verbal, sexual, and physical abuse; fear of losing their employment and the opportunity to fulfill their career dreams; fear of losing their housing; fear of living as an outsider; fear of being rejected by their church; and for some, fear of not attaining eternal life. Each gay person in attendance was experiencing the evening with deep concern for Gerry, a concern rooted in their own fears and struggles.

Gerry's partner, Randy, a handsome thirty-six-year-old with broad shoulders and thick, dark hair and a mustache, was also at the school that night. Gerry and Randy agreed that it was important for Randy to retain his anonymity. As usual, Randy and Gerry had driven separately to the meeting. Randy was standing in the hallway with a small circle of friends, his husky voice unmistakable.

Another friend approached and said, "I just heard a reporter asking some guy to point out Gerry's partner. The guy didn't know, and then the reporter asked him about Gerry's wedding ring."

All the friends instantly looked down at Randy's left hand. Bruce Wilcox, one of the men in the group, stepped toward Randy, placed both of his hands around Randy's left hand, and slowly eased the ring off his finger. Bruce carefully slid it on his own ring finger, stepped back, looked up at the others, and smiled. "We'll take turns," he said.

$$\sim$$

While the crowd waited to get into the gym, Gerry was in a meeting with his attorney, the school board, administrators, and their attorney. Gerry's attorney, William Young, had been provided by the teachers' union, the Michigan Education Association (MEA); Young specialized in labor law, and the MEA was one of his main clients. The school district's attorney, John "Patrick" White, a partner at Varnum, then one of the largest law firms in west Michigan, also specialized in labor and employment law.[14] Varnum represented numerous school districts throughout west Michigan.

School officials offered a simple solution to the controversy: Gerry would resign and they would pay him money to do so. Earlier, at an event unrelated to Gerry, a couple of school board trustees privately approached William Young and suggested that Gerry submit a written request for an audience with the board. While the opinions of individual board trustees were unclear, this appeared to be political gamesmanship. By asking Gerry to request a meeting to discuss options, these trustees created a narrative— that Gerry wanted to resign or at least was willing to resign. Once Gerry "asked" for a meeting, the trustees who wanted to pay him to leave would have leverage to pursue this approach. The school would need to come to the meeting with an offer. Another political motive underlying this approach could have been an attempt to appease those in the community, and perhaps those on the board, who wanted him fired immediately. It would create a way to argue that the better route would be to negotiate a separation agreement with Gerry.

Despite his skepticism, on December 11, a week before the board meeting in the gym, Gerry had met with the school board and administrators. Attorneys William Young and Pat White were also present.

"Do you have any questions for Mr. Crane?" Young asked.

None of the trustees responded, nor did any of them make eye contact with Gerry. The school's attorney turned toward Gerry and asked him what it would take for him to go quietly. Gerry was stunned. The attorney continued, stating that the board was prepared to pay Gerry his salary for the rest of the year.

Gerry, struggling to control his voice, said, "You have destroyed my career. I was going to teach until I was sixty. I'm now thirty-one. You crunch the numbers."[15]

Gerry rejected their offer. He was not going to be strong-armed out the door by people who despised him because of his sexual orientation.

Now, on the evening of December 18, the school was making a second effort to convince Gerry to resign. Their second offer was only somewhat better than the first. Most importantly, Gerry loved his work. He wanted to continue teaching music. He again rejected their offer.

Finally, the doors to the gymnasium opened and the crowd filed in. The bleachers on one side of the gym were opened and a standing microphone was positioned on the gym floor. As Gerry entered the gym and started making his way up the bleachers, someone yelled: "We love you, Mr. Crane!" Many stood to their feet and applauded. The chant "Ger-ry, Ger-ry" echoed throughout the gym. Students and friends walked over to Gerry and gave him words of support, a pat on the back, or a hug. Students unfurled banners and raised signs: "Hate is not a Family Value, However Love Is," "Who Are You to Judge?," and "We Must Be Reading Different Bibles." Another sign read, "We ♥ U G!" which some speculated may have a double meaning, with "G" standing for Gerry and Gay. One sign read: "Please Say No to Homosexuality." Some students wore buttons with the message, "Don't Take Our Teacher Away." Over fifty people wore royal blue ribbons, and some students wore their choral gowns and band uniforms, all in support of Gerry.

Sitting with somber, controlled expressions at tables facing the crowded bleachers were the school board trustees: Robert Kaiser, board president; Deborah Accorsi; Robert Bird; Larry Christian; David Flietstra; Tom Idema; and John Van Singel. Also seated at the table was the school's attorney, Pat White. Sitting near the front of the bleachers were the superintendent, Phil Swainston; high school principal, William Skilling; other administrators; and three student representatives.

Everyone took their places. The crowd quieted down and Board President Robert Kaiser called the meeting to order. It began as board meetings always did at this public school: with a Christian prayer offered by one of the board trustees, followed by the Pledge of Allegiance. Then the board spent ten minutes addressing other agenda items.

A trustee announced that the board was going into executive session, a closed session, "to consider dismissal or discipline pursuant to the complaints received regarding Mr. Crane." The way the trustee framed the purpose of their deliberation revealed the board's intent. The initial question for a public school board should have been whether Gerry's sexual orientation was relevant to his role as a teacher. Instead the board assumed it was relevant and moved directly to the question of whether he should be dismissed or disciplined, based on complaints that flowed from the revelation that Gerry was gay.

Public school board meetings are governed by Michigan's Open Meetings Act. Open meetings laws, also known as "sunshine laws," require public bodies to open their meetings to the public and conduct public business in the light of day. Certain topics, however, are excluded from open meetings law. For example, when a public body deliberates about personnel matters, the employee has the right to request that the discussion occur in a closed session. The decision in this case was difficult for Gerry and his attorney. A closed session, where the employee is not present, makes it easier for people to make false or unwarranted accusations when they meet privately with the board. Gerry would not be able to hear any accusations nor have the opportunity to refute them. However an open meeting meant that people could attack his character based on his sexuality and stereotypes and make false allegations—allegations that many people would assume to be true—all with the cameras running. Gerry would be humiliated in the presence of his students. His attorney opted for a closed session.

The trustees retreated to a separate room, and the crowd was left to wait. Many people gathered in small groups and shared their frustration. Others sat silently, lost in their thoughts and feelings. Some gay people attending the meeting were rightfully concerned about being outed by the media and the damage it could cause their relationships with their family and others, their reputation in their church and community, and their employment. Gerry's supporters at the meeting that night included: a gay man who held a critical job at a large, socially conservative corporation; gay professors and administrators from local colleges; and gay teachers from local school districts, including Byron Center. For these people, attending the school board meeting was in itself an act of courage.

Forty minutes passed.

An administrator at a Christian college remarked, "I cannot believe that a public school is using the Bible and religion to discriminate against the teacher."

One student asked, "Why is the debate that matters the most being conducted behind closed doors?"

The student's father agreed. "Yeah. I want to know who's saying what. If they all agreed, they would have returned by now."

Joanne Voorhees, wife of Republican state representative Harold Voorhees, also attended the meeting. Voorhees, who was active in Phyllis Schlafly's Eagle Forum, a self-described pro-family organization, described the meeting as militant.[16,17] However none of the media accounts reflected violence or threats of violence. One exception was that someone kicked a dent into the car of *The Grand Rapids Press* columnist, Ruth Butler. Butler had attended the December 4 board meeting and had written a column about it in which she called into question the actions of those who were calling for Gerry to be fired. As a regular columnist, her photo accompanied each of her published columns.[18]

As the first hour passed, the crowd's restlessness escalated. The random sighs and the different versions of "what's taking so long?" reverberated throughout the gym. Gerry's students, in an impromptu gesture, started singing "Lean On Me" and clapping. Soon others joined.

Band student Brian Jauw reflected later, "It was so hard to try to sing joyful songs while feeling so sad."

The singing continued, providing a distraction, and soothing many in the crowd.

Ninety minutes passed.

As Gerry's supporters were singing the last verse of "Amazing Grace," the trustees strode back into the gym, poker-faced. The crowd broke into instant applause.

The trustees took their seats, maintaining their rigid postures. The crowd quieted down. President Kaiser began reading the unanimous statement of the board:

> This statement is issued by the Byron Center Board of Education on December 18, 1995.
>
> The Board of Education has received considerable input and comment from the community regarding the issue of whether a homosexual teacher is a proper role model for the youth of this district, and whether such an individual should be allowed to continue to teach in this district.
>
> The Board recognizes that there are sincere and strongly held convictions on both sides of this issue. The Board is thankful for, and appreciative of the community's comments and concern.
>
> The Board wishes first to make it clear that it does not support or condone, in any manner, homosexuality as an alternative lifestyle. The Board firmly believes that homosexuality violates the dominant moral standard of the district's community. Individuals who espouse homosexuality do not constitute proper role models as teachers for students in this district.

After he spoke these words, a chorus of hissing was heard throughout the audience. President Kaiser continued:

> The Board takes its responsibility to the students and to the community very seriously. Within the constraints of the law,

the Board will take all appropriate action to protect the students of this district from immoral conduct or the encouragement or condonation of immoral conduct.

The district continues to investigate and monitor the current circumstance and controversy and will take prompt and appropriate lawful action when justified. We pray that the community will continue to provide its understanding and support, as the board continues to deal with this situation.

When he was finished, Kaiser sat down. The stunned crowd sat in silence.

Someone from the gay community shouted, "What does it mean?"

Another person yelled, "What's the answer? Does he go or do you go?"

The trustees sat stiffly, with somber expressions on their faces, and said nothing more. They had crafted, with their attorney's help, a meticulously worded statement that all trustees could support. They thought the statement was clear and needed no clarification. But the crowd's calls continued. Finally, the board president conferred with counsel and then re-read the end of the statement.

The audience continued to express anger and confusion. A woman from the gay community approached the microphone and asked the trustees to state their names and when their term of office ended, pledging to vote them out of office.

Applause erupted. The trustees sat unresponsive.

The board president announced that they would listen to individual public comments in closed session and instructed those who wanted to comment to write their name on the sign-up sheet. Each person would be called individually to talk to the board and would have up to three minutes to voice their opinion.

Many people dashed down the bleachers to the board's table to sign up. Others huddled together to discuss the board's actions or to talk with reporters.

The portion of the board's statement that had brought hissing—"Individuals who espouse homosexuality do not constitute proper role models as teachers for students in this district"—resonated with those who wanted Gerry dismissed. Many were disappointed that he was not terminated that night.

Rev. Richard Gregory agreed with the board's anti-gay proclamation, but he wanted more. "It's not over," he said.

Yet Rev. Gregory and those who shared his position understood that the board was on their side. The board's statement was explicit—homosexuals are not proper role models for students—meaning: Gerry Crane does not belong in Byron Center's school district; we want to terminate him, but we cannot do it alone; we will continue to investigate and monitor him, but we need your help. Community members left the meeting understanding their call to action.

Some who supported Gerry left the meeting feeling relieved and somewhat hopeful. Students who opposed homosexuality but supported their teacher found the board's action to be fair because despite months of controversy and pressure, the board did not fire Gerry. More people, however, were outraged.

Rev. Saunterre Irish, co-pastor of the West Michigan United Church of Christ, echoed the sentiment of gay people at the meeting that night. "Do they know that there are gay students sitting in the gym hearing this? Do they care?"

Jackie Schoon, a close friend of Gerry's who had sung at his commitment ceremony, said, "I felt so angry. There were daggers coming out of my eyes. How could they do this to such a fine teacher, a fine human being?"

As Gerry made his way through the crowd, he was engulfed

by supporters, some in tears, who hugged him while expressing words of encouragement. Reporters rushed toward him with their microphones and cameras.

"What do you think about the board's statement?" asked one reporter.

Gerry paused, gathered his thoughts, and said, "It's very offensive. There's nothing to investigate. I'm a good teacher and I'm going to stay."

"The board said they are going to monitor you. What is your response to that?" asked a reporter.

"Any other thoughts?" asked another reporter.

"I've got a concert to get ready for tomorrow night," he responded.

2

First Notes

The application and content of First Amendment principles are not determined by public opinion polls or by a majority vote.... No group, no matter how large or small, may use the organs of government, of which the public schools are the most conspicuous and influential, to foist its religious beliefs on others.

McLean v. Arkansas Board of Education
federal court case debated in 1982
during Gerry's senior year of high school

Gerald Mark Crane was born August 25, 1964, in Mount Clemens, Michigan, twenty miles northeast of Detroit. Gerry was the second of three children born to David Milton Crane and Lillian Etta Crane (née Bailey). His brother, James, was born two years before him, and his sister, Linda, was born three years after. Gerry's childhood home, a modest ranch with a brick and vinyl-sided facade, was in a well-kept neighborhood with trees and sidewalks, a mile from downtown.

Mount Clemens is located on the Clinton River, and its colorful history includes a flourishing tourist industry that started in 1873 related to their mineral baths and resorts. Tourists and celebrities would visit its twenty-three hotels and eleven mineral and bath houses. Celebrities visiting Mount Clemens' included Babe Ruth, Clark Gable, Mae West, William Randolph Hearst, Jack Dempsey, and the Vanderbilt family. By the time Gerry was born, the height of the city's mineral bath period had passed, yet remnants of the era still could be seen in the city's architecture, which includes Victorian and Italianate style mansions. For sixty years, Mount Clemens was known as the Rose Capital of the United States, an era which ended prior to World War II. At its peak, the city had ten major rose growers, with greenhouses covering over thirty acres. As late as 1976, when Gerry was twelve, Mount Clemens grew 85 percent of the state's roses.

Both sides of Gerry's family had been firmly rooted in evangelical Christian traditions for generations, and a number of his relatives were ministers: Gerry's maternal great-grandfather, Lloyd A Wilson; his great-uncle Stanley Wilson, his uncle Leonard Bailey, and his paternal grandfather, Earl M. Crane, were all Nazarene ministers, as is his cousin Matthew Bailey today; in addition, his uncle Jack Steenbergh was a Wesleyan minister.

Traditional Nazarene church doctrine required believers to abstain from alcohol, tobacco, and gambling, as well as many forms of entertainment, including dancing and going to the movies and the circus. Current Nazarene doctrine retains some of these restrictions, including abstaining from books, radio, television, and websites that involve profanity, pornography, violence, or the occult, or that "feature or glamorize the world's philosophy of secularism, sensualism, and materialism and undermine God's standard of holiness of heart and life."[19]

Gerry was raised with strong religious beliefs reflecting both Nazarene and Baptist theology. His family attended a Baptist church, and Gerry held fast to those beliefs into his early adulthood. Throughout his life Gerry looked to his Christian beliefs as he navigated life's daily demands and as he wrestled with life's larger questions.

Gerry attended public schools, and his musical talents blossomed during high school. He played piano in the Mount Clemens

Bathers jazz band, performing concerts at school and in the local shopping mall, and he played the trumpet in the concert band and orchestra. He was also a member of his high school marching band and served as drum major his senior year. He led the Battling Bathers band in "The Star-Spangled Banner" during the football game on homecoming, proudly standing on the conductor's podium, with his left hand on his hip, his right hand extended, and a whistle in his mouth. He was decked in white pants with a red stripe down the legs, cowboy boots, a white jacket with tails and red accents on the sleeves, and a red cowboy hat adorned with a solitary, white feather.

Five of the nation's most virulent anti-gay organizations were formed during Gerry's middle school and high school years: Focus on the Family was formed in 1977; the American Family Association, formerly called the National Federation for Decency, in the same year; Concerned Women for America in 1979; and Family Research Council and the Traditional Values Coalition both in 1980. These groups, which came to be known as the religious right, began to regularly demonize homosexuality and publicize false statements about homosexuals. Evangelical Southern Baptist minister Jerry Falwell Sr., who founded Liberty University, formerly Liberty Baptist College, in 1971, was one of the most influential and well-known ministers during Gerry's adolescence. In addition to proclaiming their religious belief that homosexuality was a sin, these organizations promoted the erroneous notions that homosexuals sexually abused children and recruited young people into what they described as the "homosexual lifestyle."

During Gerry's childhood and adolescence, a time when homosexuality was widely viewed as a perversion, most gay people lived closeted lives. Those who were out were typically treated as outcasts, rejected by their family and friends. It was commonplace for Randy and Gerry to hear kids and adults spew hurtful words in a tone of disgust: *Homo. Faggot. Lesbo. Pervert. Queer.*

Gay people were consistently portrayed negatively in the media and throughout American society. There were no positive gay role models, stories, images, books, magazines, or teen support groups. The limited news coverage in the popular press typically consisted of reporting the names of gay people who were arrested during police raids and sting operations. Gay characters in movies and television shows were victims of violence or ridicule, were suicidal, or were living tortured, lonely lives.[20]

In 1980, the Moral Majority helped the right wing eclipse the moderate wing of the Republican Party and nominate Ronald Reagan as their presidential candidate and propel him into the presidency. Candidate Reagan had promised to bring prayer into public schools. In January 1982 a federal court ruled in *McLean* v. *Arkansas Board of Education* that an Arkansas state law requiring the teaching of "creation science" in public schools was unconstitutional because it violated the Establishment Clause of the First Amendment.[21] The clause states that "Congress shall make no law respecting an establishment of religion." Thomas Jefferson wrote that the Establishment Clause built a wall of separation between Church and State.[22]

Later that semester, President Reagan proposed an amendment to the US Constitution permitting individual and group prayer in public schools and other public institutions; it read: "Nothing in this Constitution shall be construed to prohibit individual or group prayer in public schools or other public institutions. No person shall be required by the United States or by any State to participate in prayer."[23] While this proposal was never ratified, the Southern Baptist Convention passed resolutions supporting the amendment.[24]

During Gerry's senior year, students discussed the *McLean* case,

Reagan's proposed constitutional amendment, and related issues. In reaction to the court decision, students started carrying and reading their Bibles during school. The high school's 1982 year-book devotes two pages to these religious questions. It includes a photograph of a minister and two students huddled over a table pointing to an open book, while debating religious doctrine.

Gerry took a high school course called Bible as Literature to study the literary aspects of the Bible. It was not intended to be a Bible study. Gerry found it challenging to discuss the material without, in his mind, breaking the law.

The ease with which students brought their religious views and Bibles into their public school reflected their religious upbringing and the times. During the previous two decades, young people had been challenging authority and fighting against sexism, racism, and the Vietnam War, advocating for access to contraception, abortion rights, and gay liberation. Social change was taking place at work, at home, at school, on television, in the media, in the government, in fashion, and in advertising. Some viewed these movements as a threat to their power and privilege and to the existing social order. President Reagan's 1980 campaign slogan, "Let's Make America Great Again," resonated with conservatives yearning for a return to the cultural and political climate of the 1950s.[25]

In 1981 American doctors began documenting cases of gay men with a new disease. The scientific community first dubbed the disease "gay-related immune deficiency" and referred to it as GRID. The disease was also called the "gay cancer." Later its name was changed to "acquired immune deficiency syndrome" and called AIDS.

This was a terrifying time to be gay. Many gay people nursed their dying friends and partners, worrying that they would be next. During the early years of this disease, victims did not have a basis for hope. This disease ravaged bodies and minds, leaving its victims with tell-tale symptoms for everyone to see: emaciated bodies, skin lesions, and expressions of despondency and sorrow. Many people thought the disease could be spread through saliva, tears, or other forms of casual contact. Falwell and many others in the religious right said that AIDS was God's punishment for people who engaged in homosexuality and for a society that tolerates them. Doctors, nurses, dentists, and funeral directors often refused to serve people with AIDS. Given this connection between gay sex and death, this was also a difficult time for gay people to come out to themselves and to their families, friends, and employers. For many in the gay community, the 1980s intensified concerns about the shame, stigma, and losses associated with living an out, authentic life.

In 1982, Gerry graduated from high school as an honor student. Befitting his religious upbringing, Gerry next attended Grand Rapids Baptist College and Seminary, now Cornerstone University, where he considered a ministerial vocation.[26] Grand Rapids Baptist College, a conservative, evangelical, fundamentalist college and seminary, began in 1941 as the Baptist Bible Institute of Grand Rapids.

An active, engaged student, Gerry continued to hone his fine musical talents, playing the coronet and tuba in the Symphonic Band and the Pep Band, and singing in the Chancel Singers, a sixty-eight member choir that performed at the school's daily chapel services as well as in various cities. In a letter of recommendation, one of his music professors wrote that Gerry was "one of my most dedicated and conscientious students, and most naturally gifted.... He enjoys excellent rapport with his peers.... His genuine concern for a person is immediately apparent."[27]

Gerry was well-liked and exhibited leadership skills, serving as president of the Student Council and Chancel Singers, and as a resident assistant. Under Gerry's leadership, in 1986, the Student

Council organized a pro-life student project, raising money for the Grand Rapids Pregnancy Resource Center and the Crisis Pregnancy Center, both operated by Baptists for Life. They organized dorm competitions and fundraising events.

Gerry's college yearbook provides a snapshot of his social life—there are photographs of him playing keyboard in the Keithley Jazz Combo, shooting pool with friends, giving a classmate a haircut, attending a formal social event, and playing volleyball in the snow. His creative volleyball outfit—which included a winter jacket, hat, gloves, boots, and a pair of brightly colored, floral shorts, pulled over his jeans—earned him the caption, "Love those shorts, Gerry. PTL!" ("Praise the Lord"). In another photograph, Gerry, his head cocked to the side, eyes squinted, threw a serious look in the direction of the camera. The caption below the photo reads, "THE big man on campus—Gerry Crane."

During this time, however, Gerry struggled with his sexuality. The chasm between his religious upbringing, the Baptist College's canon, and his increasing insight into his identity produced a level of emotional and cognitive dissonance that became excruciating. He wondered how he could reconcile his emotional and sexual feelings with his religious beliefs. *Was he unworthy of everlasting life? Was he made as God intended? Would God answer his prayers for direction? Was there a way out?* Gerry traveled to a dark place. Like countless other LGBTQ+ people, Gerry attempted to take his own life. It was also at this time that Gerry came out to his parents. He endured the pain and pressed forward.

In the spring of 1986, Gerry graduated from Grand Rapids Baptist College with a bachelor of arts; he majored in music and minored in music education and speech communication. Later that year Gerry earned a second bachelor's degree in music education from Calvin College, a Christian Reformed institution in Grand Rapids.[28]

He completed a teaching internship and worked as a student teacher at Forest Hills Central Middle School and Millbrook Christian School. The professor at Calvin College who oversaw his internships wrote, "Gerry is eminently teachable. I rarely have seen a student teacher take suggestions made and apply them so effectively to his teaching." He also said that Gerry had "excellent" relations with school personnel, and that he "brings a maturity to his teaching that is uncommon for someone in his early twenties."[29] A few years later, Gerry obtained a master's degree in music education from VanderCook College of Music in Chicago.

For the next few years, Gerry worked as a part-time music instructor at four schools, two of which were Christian. Gerry's positive reviews continued during these teaching jobs. The principal at Jackson Park Junior High in the Wyoming (Michigan) Public Schools wrote that Gerry demonstrated a "sensitive focus on nurturing self-esteem which is appropriately supported with positive reinforcement, high expectations and student accountability.... [H]is instructional skills are exceptional. I would hire him in a minute if we had a full-time position open in either vocal or instrumental music."[30] At Rogers High School, also in the Wyoming district, he assisted with rehearsals and was the performance accompanist for the school's production of *South Pacific*. The director, Eleanor Keur, noted that Gerry was "especially skilled at giving students support where they needed it. He seemed to sense where the singers might falter in their key or rhythm and just at that time Gerry would play their part just a little louder so that the performer would be able to continue without making a mistake."[31]

Gerry had found his life's calling. It brought him joy and a sense of fulfillment. Armed with outstanding academic and professional credentials, his next career goal was to find full-time employment teaching music in a high school.

Gerry's purpose in life and his ethical blueprint was grounded in his religious beliefs. He searched for a religious community that aligned with his core identity as a gay man.

And he wondered if he would find love.

3

Connections

It took me many years to accept the sexual orientation I was born with, so I can understand why it is difficult for others to accept me the way I am. Acceptance of ourselves—of the way we are, of the fact that, despite our flaws, and our trials, we are all created in God's image—requires maturity and insight. Acceptance of others' differences—of diversity—requires education, setting aside our preconceptions. It requires compassion and a sense of fairness and justice.

Gerry Crane

It was a spring evening in 1990. Having finished his shift as a Pizza Hut manager in Muskegon, Randy Block drove forty miles to downtown Grand Rapids and turned down a quiet side street across from Veterans Memorial Park. He parked his car and walked toward The Apartment Lounge, a bar located in a nondescript, one-story building with a forest green cement exterior. A single gold letter "A" was painted above a small green awning that hung over a dark oak door. There were no windows in the door or in the building. The only other identifying feature associated with the bar was a sign with a small image of a beer stein and the street number.

The discreet signage and location added to The Apartment Lounge's appeal as a comfortable, safe spot for gay people to hang out and socialize, amid conservative west Michigan's otherwise stifling atmosphere. The interior decor replicated the exterior color scheme—dark oak, dim lighting, a jukebox, and a long bar—creating an intimate setting. For many gay men and lesbians in the area, their first liberating experience was the day they drove to The Apartment, parked, exited their car, and courageously approached and opened that wooden door and walked into the bar. Each step required an affirmative decision to move forward while simultaneously feeling vulnerable.

The bar was opened in 1972 by Milt Lennox and Ed Ladner, a gay couple, and is known as the oldest, continuously operating gay and lesbian bar in Michigan. Referred to as simply "The Apartment" by those in the gay community, it offered an affirming space and a place to see welcoming faces, channeling the stability of Milt and Ed's personal relationship, which lasted fifty-one years until Milt's death in 2015 at age eighty-one.

Randy walked into The Apartment around eight o'clock that night. He glanced at the row of booths and then gazed down the long, oak bar and noticed an anxious-looking man sitting alone. He immediately thought that this must be his first time in a gay bar, which he later found to be true. Randy took a seat next to him, ordered a drink, and then turned and introduced himself. He learned that the man's name was Gerry, and that he was a music teacher. They chatted and enjoyed each other's company. As the night came to a close, they left the bar together. Randy walked with Gerry to Gerry's car, pulled out a business card from his wallet, wrote his home telephone number on it, and gave it to Gerry.

"Call me if you want to get together," Randy said.

A week later Gerry called, and they made plans for their first date. Randy's job as a Pizza Hut manager required him to work nights, so they decided that, after his shift ended, Randy would pick up Gerry at his home in Grand Rapids.

On the evening they were to meet, Randy was running late, so he called Gerry. He got no answer, so he left a message: "I'll be there in forty-five minutes."

He continued driving but did not hear back from Gerry. He called him a second time. Again, Gerry did not answer. Randy left a second message: "I'll be there in a half hour."

When Randy finally arrived at Gerry's house, he noticed that Gerry's car was not in the driveway. He rang the doorbell, but there was no answer. Concluding that Gerry was not home, Randy recalled that there was a Denny's restaurant nearby. He drove to the restaurant and from there called Gerry and left a third message: "I'll be at Denny's for coffee and pie, if you want to meet me there."

After waiting for forty-five minutes, Randy went home. He'd been stood up.

Later that night Gerry called Randy and left a message: "I'm so sorry. Please call me."

Randy later discovered that a good friend of Gerry's had convinced him to attend a social event in Kalamazoo that day, telling Gerry that they would be back in time for his date. The event, however, was actually scheduled to last well after the time of Gerry's date. Adding to the delay, the friend had also asked Gerry to drive him home.

The next day when they talked by telephone, Randy gave Gerry the benefit of the doubt and said, "I'm going to the beach in Saugatuck tomorrow. Do you want to go?"

Gerry said he did.

"I'll pick you up after church," Randy said.

The next day Randy drove to Gerry's house, and they began the forty-mile journey south to Saugatuck. On the road, their conversation flowed effortlessly as they were getting to know each other. Gerry was smitten.

Saugatuck is a small beach town on the Kalamazoo River, which snakes around the town for a mile before emptying into Lake Michigan. For over a century it has been a vacation destination, attracting artists and housing successful art galleries. Saugatuck is connected to a bordering village, Douglas, by a bridge over the river. Since the late 1960s, Saugatuck-Douglas has been a well-known haven and a tourist destination for gay people, and known as one of the best gay beach towns in the Midwest.

"Where are we headed?" asked Gerry.

"Oval Beach," said Randy.

"I heard it's a den of iniquity," Gerry replied, half-joking, half-nervous.

Located on Lake Michigan, Oval Beach was known as a gay beach, where nude sunbathing was common.[32]

Gerry had never been to Oval Beach, and he tried to talk Randy out of it. Eventually Gerry agreed to try it. When they arrived, they walked along the shore holding hands, enjoying a sense of freedom and affection.

Several minutes into their walk, Gerry suddenly stopped walking and jerked back Randy's arm. "There are naked people over there."

Randy reassured him, and they continued walking, eventually finding a place to lay out on the sand.

Later, Randy fell asleep, and when he awoke, Gerry's head was resting on his chest in a manner that would later become familiar throughout the years. Their first date was a success. They both felt excited and optimistic about their new relationship.

After dating for six months, Randy and Gerry moved in together.

Randy, born in 1959, grew up in White Pigeon, a small town in southwest Michigan near the Indiana border. He was raised as a Methodist, although his family did not attend church regularly.

Unlike Gerry, Randy did not regularly hear religious messages about the dire spiritual consequences of homosexuality.

When Randy was fifteen or sixteen, he realized he was gay. He knew he could not come out to his classmates, but he knew it was equally dangerous to be outed by someone else or even be "accused" of being gay. One of Randy's household chores was to mow the lawn. While riding the tractor in the warmth of the sun during the summer before his senior year, Randy's thoughts drifted to his predicament. Based on the premise that the best defense was a good offense, he devised a plan. He set a goal of having a date with a girl every weekend. He devoted great energy to executing his plan and, to his knowledge, it provided him with his intended cover for the remainder of high school. Randy eventually became comfortable with his sexuality, and he came out to his family when he was twenty.

～

As young adults, Gerry and other gay Christian men, including Rev. Jim Lucas and Bruce Klein-Wassink, whom Gerry would meet later, were contemplating the same question: How can I reconcile my religious upbringing with my sexuality? All three men attended Calvin College. Jim Lucas, a descendant of one of the founders of the Christian Reformed Church, graduated from Calvin College in 1979, and a few years later earned a master's in divinity from Calvin Theological Seminary. Bruce, also raised in the Christian Reformed Church, earned a bachelor's degree in business and economics from Calvin in 1981, and five years later Gerry earned a degree in music education from Calvin. While they did not know each other, their paths eventually converged in the early 1990s in an affirming support group for gay Christians.

At this time most gay faculty and staff at colleges and universities were closeted at work. Yet by 1992, after he had been ordained, Jim Lucas, now Rev. Lucas, came out to some of the staff and faculty at Calvin College. That year, the Student Affairs Division at Calvin was organizing a seminar series, "Sexuality in the 90s." A Calvin employee who knew Rev. Lucas's sexual orientation asked him to speak at the seminar about homosexuality, and he agreed.

By all accounts this was the first time in Calvin College's history that an openly gay Christian Reformed Church minister spoke at a college-sponsored event. Rev. Lucas was somewhat anxious as he approached the podium to publicly share his struggles as a gay teen and young adult.

"I started writing this speech in my mind at least ten years earlier," Rev. Lucas said to the audience, "not knowing if I would ever present it to a public audience."

He continued, reading a brief passage about the biblical obligation for Christians "to release the oppressed."

"Imagine the following life experience," he said.

A child raised in a healthy Christian family, who attended a Christian high school, realized in his teens that unlike his peers, he was not romantically attracted to people of the opposite sex. This led him to have fleeting thoughts about being homosexual, a thought which was, however, too horrifying to entertain for more than a split second. As a student at Calvin College, the young man could no longer escape his romantic and sexual attraction to men, which only highlighted the number of times the audiotape in his mind played the clip that homosexuals are sick and perverse, only worthy of scornful jokes. If he was an alcoholic or drug addict, he reasoned, at least people would show some level of compassion. Having no one to talk to about these feelings, and to his knowledge never knowing or even seeing a homosexual person, he attempted to force himself to be attracted to women, a process which only led him to more frequently notice attractive men. He pled every day for God to heal him, eventually praying several times a day, all to no avail, while being reminded that society and his church reserved disdain for homosexuals, all of which left him withdrawn, feeling anxious, depressed and desperate—death began to sound like sweet relief.

Rev. Lucas paused, looked at the audience, and acknowledged that this was his own experience throughout the time he was a student at Calvin in the mid-to-late 1970s. He explained that internalized homophobia "pulses through our veins like poison—mental, emotional, and spiritual poison."

At the end of his talk, Rev. Lucas said that the "painful truth" is that the Christian church plays a significant role in continuing the oppression that gay people experience. He concluded optimistically, asserting, "We are on the brink of a new era in the church's relationship with those who are gay."[33]

As a part of their efforts to stop the progression of gay rights, the Moral Majority developed and funded organizations that sought to "cure" gay people, or in the alternative, shame them into living as heterosexuals, despite their sexuality. The term "conversion therapy," also known as "reparative therapy," refers to a variety of practices that claim to change a person's sexual orientation or gender identity or expression. It is based on the notion that the person is somehow defective, bad, or mentally ill.[34] Conversion therapy invokes feelings of disgust, shame, guilt, and confusion based on cultural and/or religious beliefs. Past techniques have included the use of drugs, electrical shock treatment, and psychological measures used in conjunction with sexual images. Current practices include the use of aversion therapy, cognitive therapy, group therapy, camps, and in-patient facilities.

Numerous organizations were formed as a part of this ex-gay movement, including Exodus International, Love in Action, The Way Out, Love Won Out, Courage International (Catholic), JONAH (Jewish), Homosexuals Anonymous, and National Association for Research and Therapy for Homosexuality, currently called the Alliance for Therapeutic Choice and Scientific Integrity. Formed in 1998, another organization, Parents and Friends of Ex-Gays and Gays (PFOX), selected a name similar to Parents and Friends of Lesbians and Gays (PFLAG), founded in 1973, a successful, affirming gay organization addressing the needs of gay people and their parents and friends.

The major medical and mental health organizations oppose the use of conversion therapy, warning that it can lead to anxiety, depression, suicide, and substance abuse.[35] Teens and adolescents, who are often forced into these practices by a parent, are also at risk of emotional and physical abuse, and homelessness. Since 2012, twenty states have adopted laws banning the use of conversion therapy for minors. New York's law also applies to adults.[36] Dozens of cities and counties have also banned conversion therapy.

One such ex-gay program, Hypernican, was founded with the stated purpose to assist gay men through the struggle of reconciling their sexuality with their religious beliefs. Hypernican's philosophy was based in part on the writings of Joseph Nicolosi, a clinical psychologist and proponent of reparative therapy. Nicolosi characterized homosexuality as a developmental problem, asserting that male homosexual attractions originated in response to the actions of their parents, and he particularly emphasized the father-son relationship. Nicolosi promoted Hypernican even though he believed that his methods would not work for all gay men.[37]

Bruce Klein-Wassink was seeing a Christian therapist to discuss issues related to his sexuality and his faith and asked his therapist about Hypernican. His therapist cautioned against attending, stating that the process could be psychologically destructive. In spite of this advice, Bruce decided to try it and form his own judgment.

On a spring day in 1992, Bruce attended his first Hypernican meeting. He drove to a generic-looking professional building, pulled his car into the lot, and noticed a man sitting alone in a parked car. Bruce drove past the car looking for a parking spot and noticed another man waiting in his car. He parked, turned off his engine, and glanced around. He saw several cars, each occupied by one man sitting alone. As the clock approached the top of the hour, the first brave man exited his vehicle and made his way to the door of the building. Slowly the others followed.

About fifteen men attended the meeting, with two men leading it. One leader explained that Hypernican's approach was to develop male bonding by reenacting the father-son relationship. He cautioned the participants that, to avoid confusion about the topic, they should only read the books and handouts the leaders provided.

"There are three levels at Hypernican," explained the group leader. "At Level 1, your job is to show up. Listen to others. You do not have to talk. When we think you might be ready for Level 2, I will interview you. Once you reach Level 2, you have an obligation to talk and contribute to our meetings. Level 3 is your goal. The reason you came here. This is a process. It will take time. Don't be discouraged."

According to the Hypernican model, at Level 3 the gay man will understand the ways his father-son relationship caused him to be gay; he will know the appropriate way to bond with men; and he will be able to live a heterosexual existence. Men participating in Hypernican were discouraged from dating or otherwise having relationships with women until after they understood how their father-son relationship caused them to be gay and after they learned the proper way to bond with men. The meetings included prayer, the presentation of materials based on Nicolosi's writings, and time for participants to share their personal struggles—these struggles were often connected to a person's religious roots. Some men remained silent. Others shared freely. One man cried at every meeting. Bruce later learned that even though some men attended the sessions for years, no one in the Grand Rapids program ever reached Level 3.

As part of the therapy, the group, along with the two leaders, gathered after the meeting for coffee at a restaurant to bond with each other in a manner that the leaders thought to be appropriate. For Bruce, and likely for others, this was the first opportunity to talk with gay men who shared their experience of attempting to reconcile their sexual identity with their religious upbringing and with other anti-gay messages in society. Finding others with shared experiences is a healthy human need. Ironically, this also facilitated gay men connecting with and socializing with other gay men.

Bruce continued to attend the weekly meetings for about six months. While he valued the opportunity to openly talk with other gay men, he concluded that Hypernican's approach was not helpful; instead, it was damaging to his spiritual growth as a Christian.

Another spiritual support group in Grand Rapids at the time was Dignity, a national organization for gay Catholics. Dignity's founding belief statement, written in 1969, reads: "We believe that homosexuality is a natural variation on the use of sex. It implies no sickness or immorality. Those with such sexual orientation have a natural right to use their power of sex in a way that is both responsible and fulfilling ... and should use it with a sense of pride." Dignity's Grand Rapids chapter was formed in 1976. Within a few years, it grew to approximately 130 members, becoming the twelfth largest chapter in the country.[38]

At roughly the same time Bruce stopped attending Hypernican, Rev. Lucas started a spiritual support group for gay Christians, which was part of a network of groups called AWARE (As We Are). AWARE was founded in 1983 in Toronto by members of a local Christian Reformed Church. Rev. Lucas's decision to form and facilitate a chapter in Grand Rapids was a natural extension of his desire to minister to gay Christians.[39]

The AWARE gatherings were held at Eastern Avenue Christian Reformed Church, a significant contrast to the nameless, nondescript, sterile office building where Hypernican meetings were held. A gay person openly walking into a place of worship—rather than surreptitiously entering an office building—created, for some, a sense of belonging and comfort. Gerry heard about the group and decided to see if it was for him. Gerry, being well-versed in Christian Reformed doctrine, found a Christian Reformed church to be a curious location for the meetings.

Rev. Lucas led the bi-weekly meetings of about twenty-five people. The two-hour sessions typically began with a discussion, and then the large group broke into small groups to discuss a specific topic. They then gathered as a whole to debrief, share news, and end with a prayer.

In 1992, Gerry was teaching band at a Christian school and knew his employment could be in jeopardy if his sexual orientation was made public. He was understandably apprehensive as he attended his first AWARE meeting. His participation that night was minimal, although he listened intently. His initial assessment of the group was positive. Gerry returned to the next meeting and soon after he brought Randy with him. Gerry soon felt at ease, opened up, shared his experiences, and started to form closer connections with others including Bruce and Rev. Lucas. In group discussions Gerry deliberated and reflected deeply on matters of faith—this was apparent to those who attended. Randy also found great value in AWARE and eventually assumed a leadership role, serving on its board of directors.

The focus of each session varied. Sometimes, they studied the theological history and interpretation of biblical passages traditionally used to condemn gay people, and at other times they discussed affirming books written from a Christian perspective. Rev. Lucas also invited guest speakers, such as local ministers. A valuable portion of each meeting was the time spent sharing and listening to each other's personal stories. Topics included "coming out to ourselves," "coming out to our families," and "coming out to friends, classmates, employers and co-workers."

Those who summoned the courage to repeatedly share their stories would eventually cross a threshold where they no longer questioned what was wrong with them and instead embraced their inherent goodness—transitioning from shame to pride. AWARE gave people the opportunity to make this transition. Some would be brought to tears while telling their own story or while hearing that someone else's loved one gave the same painful response they had encountered. The room would also fill with laughter—sometimes about painful statements that only after the passage of time can be recognized as absurd or hypocritical. The details of the stories varied, but the emotions they evoked were similar—sadness, pain, confusion, anxiety, devastation, loneliness, depression, and desperation. The list of coping mechanisms included withdrawal from family and friends, feigning an interest in people of the opposite gender, moving to a gay-friendly city, self-medication, and thoughts of and even attempts at suicide.

People discussed their struggles with family, friends, and

co-workers. Many of the most painful stories related to the holidays and other important family events. For those who had not come out to their family, the group gave them support and encouragement.

After Bruce stopped attending Hypernican, his therapist told him about AWARE. By the time Bruce started attending AWARE meetings, Gerry and Randy were regulars. Bruce discovered that he, Gerry, and Rev. Lucas shared a history at Calvin College. They had all been taught that homosexuality was not only a sin but that it was an obstacle to eternal life and redemption. According to the religion of their youth, their only option was to reject their sexual orientation psychologically, spiritually, and physically and live a heterosexual existence. The three men held strong religious convictions, and required of themselves a commitment to engage in a thoughtful, extended examination of their religion of origin.

To their mutual surprise, Gerry and Bruce learned that they had each tried Hypernican. During college and immediately after, Gerry had attended Calvary Church, an evangelical, non-denominational church located adjacent to Grand Rapids Bible College. While attending church and struggling with his sexuality, Gerry had been told about Hypernican and had attended the meetings for a short time. Independently, Gerry came to the same conclusion that Bruce had—Hypernican's philosophy and methods were destructive.

Bruce's friendship with Gerry and Randy was also important to Bruce because they were the first gay couple he had met. Bruce's experience at AWARE was transformative. He immediately noticed that people attending were psychologically healthier than those at Hypernican: they had a clearer vision of their own identity and religious convictions; they shared thoughts and experiences in a way that added value to the meetings; and they offered empathy and personal support to others in the group. They socialized often and formed fast friendships. For one and a half years, Bruce never missed a meeting. AWARE had also become an integral part of Randy and Gerry's religious and social life. Gerry had finally found a spiritually and psychologically healthy Christian home.

At this time Gerry's career was also thriving. In 1993, Gerry found full-time employment teaching band and choir. Byron Center High School had over five hundred students and was a growing community. The school's music program was weak, but as director, Gerry had the authority needed to build it. He was thrilled. The most fulfilling aspects of Gerry's life were falling into place—love, friendship, religion, and work.

4

Confidentiality Is Appreciated

Let love be genuine; hate what is evil, hold fast to what is good.
Be devoted to one another in brotherly love.
Honor one another above yourselves.
Live in harmony with one another.
If it is possible, so far as it depends on you,
live at peace with everyone.

Romans 12:9, 10, 16a, 18
Gerry and Randy's Commitment Ceremony Program

At an AWARE meeting, Gerry and Randy heard about a church with a welcoming environment for gay people. Located in downtown Grand Rapids, Westminster Presbyterian Church had a congregation of about seven hundred people, of which approximately seventy-five were openly gay. The ministers did not preach that gay people were excluded from eternal life. Instead, the church provided a spiritual community where gay congregants could be open about their sexual orientation and relationships without fear of condemnation or exclusion.

In addition to attracting people who were raised in the Presbyterian tradition, Westminster drew people from fundamentalist, evangelical, or otherwise theologically conservative backgrounds, who sought a Christian church that was more in alignment with their core religious beliefs. The church actively pursued its social justice mission, which included serving people in the downtown area who needed food and shelter.

Gerry and Randy developed a tight-knit group of friends at their new church. Westminster's Club 47—the name is a reference to the church's street address—was a group of twentysomethings and thirtysomethings who met regularly for dinners, movies, Bible study, book discussions, bowling, and other activities. Club 47 became an integral part of Gerry and Randy's social life. For some heterosexuals in the group, this was their first experience interacting with gay people who were out.

It was at Westminster that Gerry became friends with Marian Vanderwall. Marian had also attended Calvin College and had been raised in the Christian Reformed Church. Gerry and Marian had met when they both sang in a Christian Reformed choir in the mid-1980s, but Gerry had not been out to the people in that choir.

Years later, when Gerry first started attending church at Westminster, he saw Marian from afar and was immediately worried what she would think of him once she found out he was gay. After church Marian walked over to Gerry. He appeared concerned as she approached him. Marian gave Gerry a big hug and said, "I'm so happy to see you." Gerry soon learned that his concerns were unfounded. They bonded over the similar aspects of their religious journeys, and their friendship grew stronger.

Another close friendship that Gerry developed at Westminster was with Leann Arkema. Leann had grown up on the East Coast and her father was a minister in the Christian Reformed Church. She had moved to Grand Rapids to attend Calvin College, and after college she had married a minister. After seven years, their marriage ended in divorce. Devastated and broken, Leann left the church that her husband pastored and explored other churches. She started attending Westminster, and the theology and sense of community resonated with her. She eventually decided it was time to attend a membership meeting.

Arriving late to the meeting, Leann opened the door and saw that everyone was seated with their backs to her. As she hesitantly stepped into the room, feelings of fear and loneliness washed through her body. She thought about leaving, but a young man seated many rows away turned around, saw her, and immediately motioned for her to come and sit by him. Leann followed the man's invitation and took a seat.

"Hi, I'm Gerry. This is Randy," he said, pointing to the man next to him.

They exchanged greetings.

After the meeting, Gerry and Randy invited Leann to join them for lunch. She learned that Gerry had also been raised in a conservative faith and that they shared a strong devotion to their Christian faith. They developed a deep friendship.

A few years later, Leann reminded Gerry of the day they first met. "You were facing the front of the room, and Rev. Bill was ready to start the meeting. Why did you turn around and look at the door?"

"God whispered to me that there was someone in the back of the room who needed a friend," Gerry responded.

Thinking about that painful time in her life and how the three of them would get together regularly for dinner, Leann said, "Gerry and Randy scooped me up in my time of great need. They were my first gay friends."

⌒⌒

Gerry and Randy had purchased a house on Ethel Street, in southeast Grand Rapids. Built in 1915, it reflected the American Foursquare style of that era. The house was in walking distance of the local gay and lesbian community center, The Network. Their neighborhood was also home to the city's gay coffeehouse, Sons & Daughters. The business was opened in April 1990 by Jeffery Swanson and his partner, Dennis Komac. Jeff and Dennis moved to Grand Rapids from California when Dennis was hired as director/curator of the Grand Rapids Art Museum. Their coffeehouse sold gay- and lesbian-themed magazines, books, greeting cards, jewelry, rainbow flags, bumper stickers, buttons, shirts, and other pride items. At this time most bookstores did not carry any gay-themed books or magazines, let alone have an entire section devoted to the material. Most importantly, Sons & Daughters served the pressing need for an affirming public space, where gay people could enjoy coffee and dessert or shop with a sense of dignity and belonging. The atmosphere was infused with a feeling of kinship and "family," the colloquial term used by gay people at the time to describe others who shared their identity.

Gerry had refined taste and took pride in their house. One day Randy decided to surprise Gerry by painting their dining room olive green and solicited Leann's help. She thought this was a terrific idea, and the two of them spent a day painting the room while Gerry was at work. They completed the task and waited expectantly for Gerry's arrival and reaction. When he returned home, Gerry was not pleased.

Lashing out at Leann, he exclaimed, "Don't ever let Randy pick the colors!"

This was classic Gerry—interior design was *his* domain.

Gerry and Randy's Ethel Street home became the scene for many dinner parties and other social gatherings. These celebrations included delicious food, friendly conversation, and captivating entertainment.

Gerry entertained his guests by playing classical music, show-tunes, and holiday sing-along songs on his polished, black grand piano—the crowning piece of their living room. Known for his spot-on impersonations, evenings would often include two of his favorites—The Church Lady from Saturday Night Live and Ethel Merman singing "There's No Business Like Show Business." At one of their themed parties, guests were asked to come dressed as a person who would be found in "Baptist Hell." Those attending included a pregnant nun, an anti-gay minister, and Joan Crawford, wire hanger in hand. A female goddess Christina, dressed in white, played the harp in a corner of the room.

Gerry and Randy also hosted Thanksgiving dinner, inviting other "holiday orphans"—gay friends who were estranged from their family of origin or otherwise not welcome—along with others who did not have holiday plans.

In August 1994, Gerry's friends threw a surprise party to celebrate his thirtieth birthday. Some came dressed as members of the 1970s disco group the Village People, including a cowboy, police officer, sailor, and construction worker. At the party, they approached Gerry, escorted him to a chair facing them, turned on their boom box, and performed a choreographed dance while lip syncing to "Macho Man." When it ended, Gerry spontaneously got up, ran toward their dance line, jumped in the air, and landed horizontally in their arms.

⌒⌒

"I've been planning my death," Gerry said to Leann.

"What?" asked Leann.

"No, really. I've talked to an attorney."

Gerry worried that if he were to develop serious health problems, his biological family would appear and, in an effort to save him spiritually, assume legal authority to make medical decisions and prevent Randy from having hospital access. It was a common fear for gay people. Families often refused to acknowledge the legitimacy of those relationships. Since marriage was not legal, a gay person's parents or siblings held the legal right to make end-of-life decisions. There were a host of horror stories where a gay person's family of origin would swoop into the hospital, assert familial rights, and deny the gay person's partner access to their loved one and to medical information. For this reason, it was common for gay people to hire an attorney to draft legal documents conveying those rights to their partner, or to a heterosexual person, who respected their relationship and had the ability and willingness to stand-up to anti-gay parents or siblings.

In addition, Gerry thought if he named Randy as his patient advocate—the person legally designated to make health care decisions in the event of temporary or permanent incapacitation—his family would feel even more empowered to interfere. To quell his anxiety, Gerry selected two close friends to serve as his patient advocates: Leann Arkema and Chris Gibbie.

As part of this process, Leann was required to sign a document stating she voluntarily accepted the role of patient advocate. Gerry handed Leann the document. She read it, paused, looked at Gerry, and said, "I'll sign this on one condition—that we will still have this when we are ninety years old, sitting next to each other in rocking chairs. Don't make me use this before."

Gerry smiled and nodded.

⁓

Most of 1995 was a joyous time for Gerry. His relationship with Randy was thriving, and he had a vibrant social life anchored by heartfelt friendships. He was deeply passionate about his work, and had found a spiritually sustaining religious community that included like-minded believers with whom he could engage in ongoing dialogue and growth.

In the summer of 1995, Gerry and Randy traveled to Boston to attend the commitment ceremony of gay friends. They found the ceremony to be meaningful and moving. Soon after, they decided to formalize their five-year relationship by pledging their love for each other.

A commitment ceremony did not have legal significance. It did not create legal rights or responsibilities. At the time, the State of Michigan did not permit either civil unions or same-sex marriage. For Gerry and Randy, a commitment ceremony would provide a validating, momentous way for them to exchange formal vows in the presence of loved ones.

They immediately selected a date—October 21, 1995. In July, Gerry started planning the music. He had two criteria in mind when selecting musicians: their talent and their ability to keep the details of the event confidential. He asked Jackie Schoon, his good friend from Club 47 at Westminster, to be the vocalist. And he asked a woman he trusted to play as a part of a string quartet. Unfortunately, she had a scheduling conflict, so instead Gerry selected a violinist and pianist to round out their musical repertoire.[40]

The senior minister of Westminster Presbyterian Church at that time was Rev. William Evertsberg, an inspiring speaker with a compelling personality. Rev. Bill—as he was known to congregants—hailed from Grand Rapids, was raised in the Christian Reformed Church, and graduated from Calvin College. In his early adult years his theological beliefs changed. After attending Princeton Theological Seminary he was ordained in the Presbyterian Church. He began serving at Westminster in 1990. According to Rev. Bill, there are two important roles for a minister: to serve as a prophet, or truth-teller, prioritizing truth and justice, and to serve as a minister, caring for people. It was in his role as a prophet that Rev. Bill preached a series of sermons on sexuality titled, "The Homosexual Christian," proclaiming that homosexuality is consistent with Christianity. And it was in his role as minister that Rev. Bill agreed to officiate Gerry and Randy's ceremony. They were elated. Next, Rev. Bill had Gerry and Randy begin pre-marital counseling—the same type he required of heterosexual couples.

⌒⌒

With many of the details in place for the ceremony, Gerry antic-ipated a joyful, fulfilling year as he returned to school in August. On his first day back, however, Gerry was told to report to the administration building. He had no idea about the purpose of the meeting. When he arrived, two people were waiting for him: Assistant Superintendent of Personnel Robert Wait and Principal William Skilling. They told Gerry that they knew that he was a homosexual and that they had heard he was planning to marry a man. Wait said that the school board president, Bob Kaiser, had received similar complaints. Skilling added that others had raised "the issue" in the past.

Gerry was stunned. How did they know about his commitment ceremony? He and Randy had been careful about who they told. He did not know how to respond. He had no time to take this in or to think what, if anything, to say. Gerry asked if he needed an attorney. Wait said that was not necessary—they were simply informing him about the complaints because they were required to do so under his union contract.

"What are you going to do about it?" Gerry asked.

Wait said they did not plan on doing anything and that they hoped that "the situation will blow over."

The administration had not, in fact, complied with their require-ment to inform Gerry about a complaint received the previous school year. In April 1995, a mother had called Skilling and had asked him if Gerry was gay. Skilling told her that he "had no evidence of him being gay." The parent then said that a senior student, whom she named but who was not her child, may be gay because he spent time around Gerry. Skilling told her that he "saw no evidence of that either," adding, "I will keep my eyes open to any possibility."

Skilling's response was inappropriate. He should have told the parent that he could not discuss a teacher's private life. Skilling should also have protected the student's privacy. He should have told the caller that he could not discuss personal matters about students other than her own children. By telling her that he would keep his eyes open to the possibility, he implied that it *is* her business and that he also thought it would be problematic if the student were gay. The parent did not allege that Gerry did anything improper. The supposed problem was based on their shared religious belief that homosexuality was wrong and their false notion that a student could become gay by being around a gay teacher. The principal clearly thought this was a serious matter because he told the parent he needed to keep his eyes open to this issue.

It was this same mother who called Principal Skilling in August and asked if he knew that Gerry was getting *married* to a man. Skilling told her that he did not know anything about it, and that again he had no "evidence" about him being gay. A few days later, a parent who worked at the high school called him with the same questions. The parent told Skilling that her son no longer wanted to stay in band class because his teacher was a homosexual. Skilling told her that he did not have "evidence" of Gerry being gay and that another parent had called with the same complaint. He explained that he told the other parent that he "would be watching to see if it were true."

In April and August, Skilling spoke to parents about not having "evidence" and about his intent to watch to see if these aspects of Gerry's private life were true. However, it was not the principal's job to gather intelligence about a teacher's sexuality to serve the wishes of parents. His continual use of the word "evidence" sent a message—if he had evidence, he might do something about it.

Gerry left the August meeting shocked that people in Byron Center knew about his upcoming commitment ceremony. They had invaded his privacy. Administrators had told him that the school district did not plan to take action against Gerry, but they premised that answer on their hope that it would "blow over." What did that mean? What if it did not "blow over"? Equally disturbing was the tone of their voices and what they did not say. He heard contempt, not compassion. They offered no support. They did not say they would protect his right to a private life. They did not say that his job was *not* in jeopardy. His future would depend on the direction and intensity of the winds in Byron Center.

Gerry told Randy about the meeting. Randy shared Gerry's outrage. They sought input from trusted friends and from Rev. Bill; all were disturbed by this news. Gerry and Randy also consulted with attorneys, who told them that Byron Center could fire Gerry based on his sexual orientation because neither Michigan law nor federal law prohibited discrimination based on a person's sexual orientation. If fired for that reason, Gerry could file a lawsuit arguing that discrimination based on his sexual orientation violated his constitutional rights under the Equal Protection and Due Process clauses of the Constitution; but that process would take years, and the odds of success were minimal.

On September 7, Gerry sent a memo to the principal requesting details about each complaint, including the date and names of those who contacted him. Gerry also asked what the administration intended to do. Skilling replied the next day in writing that he did not have written documentation about "the conversations I had with parents concerning your lifestyle," adding that they had requested anonymity. Skilling wrote that because the parents did not file formal complaints, "the district would regard them as unsubstantiated rumors" and that "the district plans to do nothing at this time."

Skilling's statement about not documenting the conversations was disingenuous, at best. Later, in 1996, Skilling prepared a document titled "Documentation of Gerry Crane" in which he detailed the April and August 1995 telephone conversations with parents. He had included the names of the parents, the date and time of the calls, and the name of the student who the parent said was gay.

Further, Skilling's response to Gerry is telling. He framed the conversations as being about Gerry's *lifestyle*. The memo is also telling for what it did not say. It did not acknowledge Gerry's excellent work as a teacher. The district did not express their intent to defend his right to continue teaching regardless of other people's religious or political views about his sexual orientation.

Complaints from parents about the marriage rumor continued for the next six weeks. Skilling later wrote that he told parents who called in September and early October that he was "not able to discuss the personal life of any staff member." It is likely that he adopted this response after consulting with the district's attorney. He could not however take back his earlier comments to parents; his expressed intent to watch for information about Gerry's personal life signaled Skilling's belief that Gerry's sexuality was relevant to his teaching. Skilling attended the same church as some of the parents who were complaining. His constant refrain that he lacked "evidence" become a call to action for these parents.

Meanwhile, Gerry and Randy wondered whether they should proceed with their ceremony. Gerry thought of the painful and arduous journey he had taken to live a personally and spiritually authentic life. He had taken precautions to keep his private life out of the school setting—a sacrifice which took a toll on him. He could not, however, let his employer or the parents of his students impose their religious beliefs on his personal life. Gerry and Randy's desire to have their commitment ceremony officiated by their minister was borne of their deeply held Christian beliefs. Those who were condemning him were interfering with his right to exercise those beliefs. Gerry and Randy decided to move forward with their plans.

~~

Gerry and Randy had planned to hold their ceremony in Westminster's sanctuary. Getting approval, however, was complicated. The church's board would need to confer and approve the use of the sanctuary for the same-sex commitment ceremony. Many members of Westminster believed that affirming the spiritual lives of gay people was critical to the church's mission. Other parishioners, however, believed that homosexuality was a sin and contrary to the Bible. Yet Gerry and Randy believed they would have sufficient support on the board, which consisted of twenty-two members.

Cognizant of the role he held as the senior minister of a congregation that held mixed views regarding homosexuality, Rev. Evertsberg informed members of the congregation of his intent to be the officiant at Gerry and Randy's commitment ceremony. The response was mixed, with many members expressing their disapproval and even outrage. However, as a pastor ordained by God, Rev. Evertsberg had the freedom to make his own decision about participating in their ceremony if it were held outside of the church. After hearing about the congregation's reactions, Gerry and Randy selected an off-site venue—Frederik Meijer Gardens.

"They made this decision in an attempt to protect their church and my job," Rev. Bill said later.

Gerry and Randy invited a hundred people to their ceremony. The list consisted of people they loved *and* who loved them unconditionally and supported their union. They selected a simple, elegant invitation with a sketch of a single rose on the cover. The invitation began:

> The ultimate miracle of love is this
> that love is given to us
> to give to one another

The lower left corner of the invitation included the words "confidentiality is appreciated."

The third Saturday of October arrived. As guests turned into the Frederik Meijer Gardens, they drove down a long, winding entrance, bordered by rows of well-manicured trees and flowers. The botanical garden, which had opened earlier that year, featured a tropical conservatory, gardens, and nature trails. The main building contained indoor gardens, as well as rooms for exhibits and events. Guests walking toward the building entrance breathed in the crisp air, while surrounded by Michigan's brilliant autumn colors.

In the room were round, cloth-covered tables decorated with flowers and candles. Soon the room was filled with Gerry and Randy's friends, some who had become their family, and all who supported and celebrated their relationship.

As the pianist and violinist played "Méditation" from the opera *Thaïs*, composed by Jules Massenet, the two grooms entered dressed in black tuxedos. Guests were asked to light the candles during the processional as the grooms approached each table.

With the candles lit, the vocalist sang "The Ones Who Aren't Here," a song written in 1981 by a gay man, John Calvi, and first recorded by lesbian musician Meg Christian. The song was often played at LGBTQ+ memorials, weddings, and AIDS events. The last verse reads,

> So let's pass a kiss
> and a happy sad tear
> and a hug the whole circle round
> for the ones who aren't here
> for the hate and the fear
> for laughter, for struggle, for life.
> Let's have a song here for me and for you
> and the love that we cannot hide.
> And let's have a song
> for the ones who aren't here
> and won't be coming out tonight.[41]

After readings from the Old Testament and the New Testament, the soloist, their friend Jackie Schoon, sang "On Eagles' Wings." Gerry and Randy affirmed their love, recited their vows, and exchanged gold rings. Jackie took in their look of mutual adoration and commitment and thought, *God's grace is so great.*

The ceremony was followed by a catered dinner, with violin music playing throughout the meal. For most guests, even those who were themselves gay, this was the first commitment ceremony they had attended. Many commented that it was one of the most meaningful, elegant, and delightful ceremonies they had experienced. At the end of the night, with a handful of people left in the room, Leann, one of the Guest Attendants, remembered something odd that had happened earlier in the evening. She told Gerry and Randy that before the ceremony began, she had observed a young man enter the back of the room, pick up a program, turn around, and leave. It struck her as curious, but the processional was about to begin, and her attention was needed elsewhere.

5

Ring

I have enriched the lives of my students for these past ten years: brought them an appreciation for music, honed their skills and artistry, developed cohesive teamwork among members of my choirs and bands. I have taught with compassion and skill, and through example, I hope I have imparted to my students my own values for education, honesty, God, community, and a work ethic.

Gerry Crane

Gerry received a telephone call. It was the day after his commitment ceremony.

"Mr. Crane, you won't believe what's going on," said one of his students in a fast-paced, distressed voice. "They're passing copies of this church program about you getting married to some guy.... They're passing it around town."

Gerry assured the student. "Don't worry. It'll be OK."

Gerry received a few more calls that afternoon with similar messages—one from a parent and one from another student. They were all concerned for Gerry.

While Gerry tried to reassure the callers, in fact he was devastated by the news. The program for his and Randy's ceremony had been written for the eyes of the people who loved them. It was personal. It was symbolic—a keepsake. It contained details of their sacred ceremony—details that reflected the deep religious beliefs of Gerry, Randy, and those in attendance. The thought of his students' parents passing it around the community, and talking about it with contempt and ridicule, was at once infuriating and humiliating.

As a teacher, Gerry could not take time off in the middle of October for a honeymoon. He did, however, take a personal day on Monday. On Tuesday, as he drove to school, he did not know what to expect. He couldn't complain or even discuss how to handle this with his colleagues, many of whom attended churches with anti-gay beliefs. Gerry's most important concern was his students. What did they know? What did they think? How did they feel?

As his first class began, a student held up her hand. Gerry called on her.

"Mr. Crane, what did you do this weekend?"

Gerry did not respond.

She continued. "What's that on your finger?"

"It's a ring," Gerry said.

The student persisted. "Does it mean anything?"

"It was a gift from a friend." He attempted to move the students' attention to the material for the day.

Throughout that week, students continued to make comments and ask questions. Many students were supportive. Some expressed disapproval—homosexual relationships violated their Christian beliefs. Others were confused. They knew their teacher was being criticized but did not know why. This led some to think that he must have done something seriously wrong.

Parents started calling the school to complain and request that their children be removed from Gerry's class. While his commitment ceremony was the triggering event, many of the complaints were couched in terms of Gerry's sexuality. They did not want their children being taught by a homosexual.

By midweek, Gerry was called into a meeting with Skilling and Vice Principal Robert Noordeloos. Gerry's union representative,

David Prindle, also attended. Prindle, a science teacher at Byron Center High School, served as the president of the Byron Center Education Association (BCEA). It was in that capacity that he served as Gerry's local union representative, whose role is to explain to employees their union rights and update leadership about the status of local issues.

During the meeting administrators told Gerry that they knew of his commitment ceremony and that parents had been calling the office to complain. Some demanded that their children be removed from his class. Others threatened to do so if he remained as the teacher. Skilling explained that the superintendent and the district's attorney instructed him to honor requests from parents to remove their children if their requests were based on religious convictions. Gerry said that teaching tolerance is an important goal in education. Skilling said that he believed parents had a right to decide who their children have as a teacher. Skilling's comment was misguided. While parents may give schools their input, parents do not have an absolute right to select their children's teachers.

Gerry said that he had not told anyone at school that he was gay or that he was having a commitment ceremony. He said he would try to circumvent the issue but that if people continued to press him, he would not lie.

Gerry asked, "What should I do if parents call me at home?"

They gave him no directions. The vice principal said simply, "No one called me when I got married."

Gerry left the meeting feeling vulnerable. It was clear that no one had his back.

The next few weeks were chaotic. Gerry and David Prindle were meeting almost daily to discuss the latest complaint or attend a meeting with administrators. They had to use their classroom preparation hour for these meetings.

Parents were calling the school, demanding to have their children removed from Gerry's class. Most demanded his dismissal because he was homosexual, and a smaller number focused on what they described as his marriage to another man. Homosexuality violated their Christian beliefs; therefore, he was an improper role model for their children.

Allegations were made that Gerry said something in class in an inappropriate manner. One mother called to complain that Gerry said to her daughter's choir class, "Rumors are flying around. Yes, I am gay and it is none of your business. I married another gay."

Skilling talked to the student later that day. According to the student, Gerry had actually said, "The rumors are true, but my personal life is my business. You guys should think about what you are saying."

The student's mother later told the principal that she wanted her daughter removed from Gerry's class regardless of what her daughter wanted to do.

Since Gerry was the only music teacher at the school, students removed from his class would no longer be part of the school's music program. Gerry felt bad for the students. He believed in the value of music education. Students had been playing their instrument for years. Some wanted to continue their music education in college. Why would their parents do this to them?

The controversy disrupted classes and created confusion for the remaining students. Which one of their classmates would be pulled out today? Band and choir are team endeavors. Each student has a specific role—an instrument, a place to stand in the marching band, a voice to bring to the choir. When would this stop? Who would be left?

Not surprisingly, students continued to talk among themselves, bringing their concerns and questions into the classroom. What was going on? Why was their teacher, who was valued by students and parents alike, under attack? While some parents discussed Gerry's homosexuality with their children, others did not.

Gerry wanted to tell his students that they needed to focus on their education, not his personal life. At the same time, he needed to protect himself from false accusations. To this end Gerry eventually brought an audio recorder to school. At the start of each class that day, he turned on the recorder and talked to his students. "I know you've heard rumors about me. You have to ask yourself two things: Is it true? And, should it matter? If not, then I have a job to do, and you have a job to do. Let's get to it."[42] Gerry did not use the words "gay," "homosexual," or "married." His message was clear. His personal life was not a topic for discussion at school. The students respected him. They knew it was time to get to work.

Around the same time, Gerry talked to Robin Langley of the Michigan Education Association (MEA), the statewide union for teachers. She told Gerry that she had alerted the MEA's attorney about what was happening to him and assured him that the MEA would come down hard on the district if they violated his rights. She told him to call her immediately if anything occurred. He was pleased with the MEA's verbal support. He knew, however, that the situation was more complicated than that. Parents were using his personal life to denigrate him as a teacher. He did not have the type of legal protection that was needed, and school officials were not on his side.

The school's parent-teacher conferences were held in early November. This was the first time he would meet with parents since his personal life had become the talk of the town. While sitting at conferences waiting for parents to arrive, Gerry wrote a letter to a former student who had enlisted in the Army. Gerry began: "I'm a low-down, rotten, gutter-licking, old, decrepit piece of s#@t for not writing to you…. I truly apologize and will try to be better at this 'communication thing.' … I think you've really stepped out to chart new territory for yourself, and you should be proud of your accomplishments. I'm really happy that your health held up, and you were able to stick with your Army plans. I thought of you many times and prayed for you often."

Gerry told his former student about what he referred to as a "stupid stunt." Earlier that day a student rode his motorcycle through the hallway. Gerry also told him that in the previous three weeks, thirty-one students had dropped his classes. He shared his general frustrations, but emphasized how much he appreciated the support of some students.

During the conferences, a person from the First Reformed Church of Byron Center approached Gerry and handed him a letter. It was from the consistory of the church and was printed on church stationery, which listed Rev. Dr. Jack Doorlag as the church's pastor. The letter, dated November 6, 1995, addressed to "Mr. Crane" read in part: "As spiritual leaders in our church and community, we are deeply concerned about what we have discovered in the past couple of months about your lifestyle…. We hope you will reconsider the lifestyle you have chosen to follow. It is our prayer that you will consider the eternal consequences of your decisions even as we must do the same as spiritual leaders."

The letter stated that the consistory planned to send a letter to the school board before its November 20 meeting. They asked Gerry to either meet with them or to send them a response to their letter. Gerry did neither.

The school received letters and telephone calls about Gerry on almost a daily basis. Most people called to complain about Gerry, to demand to have their children removed from his class, or to call for the school to terminate his employment. Parents accused Gerry of talking to their son or daughter about their decision to remove their child from his class. Students talked to Gerry, telling him that they were upset because their parents were making them drop out of his class. Some students were in tears when they returned their band uniforms to Gerry. They felt bad about the way he was being treated.

The principal repeatedly called Gerry to the office, presenting him with what became the complaint of the week, and at times, of the day. On one such day the mother of one of Gerry's students called the principal to complain that Gerry had used inappropriate language in the classroom. The parent reported that Gerry told the class that they were "acting like a bunch of jackasses." She said he also said, "I know you girls are on the rag, but you don't need to be crabby about it," and that when he was instructing students during warm-up breathing exercises he had said, "I don't want to see your boobs."

Skilling met with Gerry to discuss the complaint. Gerry explained that a group of students were punching each other and throwing things. Gerry instructed them to report to the vice principal's office and said, "You people need to start behaving like young adult freshman rather than a bunch of jackasses."

As for the next comment, Gerry said that a group of girls were acting up. One of the girls said that they were "on the rag." Gerry responded, "I don't need to hear about you being on the rag." Finally, Gerry explained that while he was demonstrating breathing exercises, he placed his hands on his chest and told them that he wanted to see their stomachs come out, not their chests. One girl said, "You mean our boobs?" Gerry responded, "Yes, I don't want to see your boobs."

Skilling told Gerry that he should not be using the student

jargon. Gerry agreed. He said he would speak to his class about it the next morning and that he would call the student's mother and explain what happened.

On another day in early November, Gerry was told to meet with his principal. Vice Principal Noordeloos and Gerry's union representative, David Prindle, were also at the meeting. The first topic was a discussion about the students who were being removed from Gerry's classes.

"My job is to teach. Professionally, I need to know who is leaving my class and why. I need to know as soon as they're out," Gerry said.

Gerry asked about rumors he was hearing: "Are students being asked if they would stay in music if there was another teacher? If this is being fed from this school, it's inappropriate. I'll take legal action if that's the case."

The principal told Gerry that "we" never made that comment. It was not clear who he was including in the word "we."

Gerry asked about one of the school guidance counselors, Brian Fiddle. "I heard that Brian was asking this question. What's being said when students are taken out of my class?"

Skilling said they tell parents that the administration cannot speak about anybody's personal life.

"I've received calls from Rev. Gregory from Byron Center Bible Church and Pastor Dobson from Calvary Church," said Gerry. Gerry had attended Calvary Church during and immediately after his college years. "Pastor Doorlag gave me a letter," Gerry added. "Is the school providing information to them?"

The assistant principal said he did not provide any information.

"What is the district doing to put this to rest?" asked Gerry. "The district needs to be proactive instead of reactionary."

The principal said that the school was caught between a rock and a hard place. He further explained that the parents had the right to determine the classes their kids took if their religious beliefs were being infringed upon. He said that this was the same as a parent's decision to prohibit their child from sex education information.

The principal's comment about sex education was not analogous to a parent demanding to have their child removed from a class because of the teacher's sexuality. Sex education is about course curricula, and Michigan law gives parents the right to opt out. However, in this case, parents were demanding that their children be pulled from Gerry's class because of their opinion about his personal life—not course content.

The principal praised Gerry, stating that he was a good teacher and that no one could argue with that. He added that Byron Center was a conservative community and that its people hold certain moral convictions.

The vice principal said they couldn't debate scripture with parents, and asked Gerry if he had any suggestions.

"It's not my job to solve this problem," Gerry said. He paused and added, "There should be diversity or sensitivity training."

Gerry was correct. It was the administrators' job to handle school controversies. They needed to set the tone and establish boundaries. A part of any solution, however, would have required school officials to publicly support Gerry.

Vice Principal Noordeloos explained that their situation was especially difficult because Gerry was the only music teacher at the school. He continued to explain that they had an idea—that they might bring in another music teacher who would co-teach with Gerry.

This was not a solution. It would keep the spotlight on Gerry. Students would know why a second teacher was added to their classroom. The implication would be that the school and parents did not trust Gerry to be alone with his students. It would humiliate Gerry and take away his authority and creative freedom. It was a disguised effort to appease parents in the short term with the hope that Gerry would eventually resign.

The principal heard that Gerry had spoken to his classes about this situation, and he asked what Gerry had told them.

Gerry explained what he had said, adding, "I recorded it. You can have a copy if you want." The vice principal said that it was illegal to record conversations. Gerry had only taped his own statements to his students.

"How are you preparing for the November 20 school board meeting?" Gerry asked.

Skilling said that they were going to follow their attorney's advice.

Gerry said he would attend the meeting with representation.

The vice principal's statement that the school could not debate scripture with parents was a smoke screen. Gerry and his supporters never argued that the school should have debated scripture with parents. To the contrary, they argued that interpretations of scripture had no place in a public school's evaluation of a teacher.

The "religious reason" standard used by the school, as it was applied to Gerry, arguably violated constitutional law. The Establishment Clause of the First Amendment prohibits the government from adopting laws "respecting an establishment of religion." The government cannot adopt policies or practices which favor one religion over another.

The Free Exercise clause of the First Amendment prevents the government from interfering with a person's freedom to exercise their own religious beliefs. It does not, however, give parents the right to insist that public school teachers share the parents' personal religious beliefs. Even if it did, Gerry and many who supported him were also Christian. Within Christianity, people carried different views about many social issues, such as the use of birth control, abortion, and women as clergy. Gerry believed that homosexuality was compatible with Christian theology—a belief that was shared by other Christians in west Michigan and throughout the country.

The application of the Free Exercise and Establishment clauses in public schools has been and continues to be debated in the courts. The issues in these cases have focused on school prayer, student clubs, curriculum, student expression, religious holidays, the Pledge of Allegiance, and meals served in the cafeteria. Parents neither have a right to demand that their children be taught by heterosexual teachers nor a right to insist that their children be taught by teachers who practice their religious beliefs.

The campaign to terminate Gerry's employment continued to grow and gather steam. It consumed an increasing amount of his time and energy. Gerry, however, was determined to remain focused on his work. November and December are an especially busy time for music teachers. While the football season had recently ended, Gerry continued working with the marching band. He had entered the group in the Grand Rapids Santa Claus Parade. On the morning of Saturday, November 18, students went to downtown Grand Rapids and lined up for the parade. At the end of the day, Byron Center won the parade's "Best Band" award. Gerry was proud of his students.

When he returned to work on Monday, the students were still excited about their performance. His chance to relish his students' achievement, however, would be cut short that day.

The school had arranged for Rev. Peter Marshall to speak at a student assembly on that Monday, November 20, the same day as the board meeting. A local organization of parents and ministers called Concerned Citizens of Byron Center planned the event. Marshall, a nationally recognized conservative Christian evangelist, was associated with an organization called Restoring Our Heritage.

During one of the previous meetings with the principal and vice principal, Gerry had asked about this student assembly, "Is he going to talk about homosexuality and the downfall of the family?" Gerry received no response.

In a talk at the Christian Coalition's "Road to Victory" conference in October 1995, Rev. Marshall had said that "America is God's project. He willed it into existence. It's a divine experiment in self-governance." He further alleged that the "great rallying cry of the Revolution" was "No King but King Jesus." He asserted that the intent of America's founders was "to found a just society based on the Bible."[43] On the contrary, the United States was founded on what Thomas Jefferson called "a wall of separation between church and state."[44]

Gerry attended the assembly that day. Rev. Marshall told students that they needed to understand the "biblical basis" of American life, and he drew a parallel between "Christ and the cross" and the actions of the patriots at Valley Forge, stating that the patriots, like Christ, chose to stay and endure rather than leave.

Rev. Marshall discussed his ideas about the meaning of American freedom. It is not, he declared, the freedom to go out and use others sexually nor is it the freedom to get AIDS. He told these *public school* students that the call of God's people is to live by biblical principles. He concluded by proclaiming that America needed to return to its original moral and spiritual values. His comment about the freedom to get AIDS clearly played into religious and cultural fears and stereotypes: that AIDS was a gay disease; that the vast majority of gay men had AIDS; and that the Christian God created AIDS to punish gay men and a society that had accepted homosexuality.

The school's intent was clear. On the day of the first board meeting about Gerry, the administrators had required students to listen to a minister proclaim that homosexuality was against "biblical principles" and the American way of life.

Some parents were furious. The connection between this event and the school board's ongoing debate about Gerry's sexuality was unmistakable. The next day, Principal Skilling sent a memorandum to the faculty. Rev. Marshall's talk, he wrote, went beyond the bounds and parameters given to him. The principal said that he had told him that he could only discuss "who our Founding Fathers were and how their faith influenced the development of our current government." He had told Rev. Marshall that he "could not proselytize Christianity." Rev. Marshall had told the principal that his intent was to give students "history lessons that were not taught anymore in our schools."

Concerned Citizens' intent, the principal added, was to bring a celebration of our nation's heritage around Thanksgiving time. In his memo the principal defended the president of the group—she had reported that she warned Rev. Marshall about the limits of his talk, and she apologized to the principal for the content.

Skilling's mea culpa and explanatory memo glossed over the heart of the matter. Why did the principal approve bringing a conservative Christian evangelist speaker to talk to students amid a public, religious-based attack against one of his most talented teachers? It is unlikely that the principal would have authorized this event without knowing Rev. Marshall's views and work. Further, if he was not familiar with Rev. Marshall's views, he had an obligation to read about him before having students listen to an American history talk by a minister.

~~~

The school board meeting was held that evening, November 20, a month after Gerry's commitment ceremony, and a month before the December 18 meeting. A typical school board meeting drew about a dozen people. This one drew more than one hundred, including students, parents, and others in the community. Over thirty people placed their names on the sign-up sheet at the start of the meeting to give comments. After discussing and voting on other agenda items, the board met in a closed session to discuss what, if anything, they were going to do about the gay teacher. One-by-one those who signed up went into a conference room to speak to the board.

The media was also there. Some students, in an effort to protect Gerry, had contacted local television stations. Journalists interviewed students and parents, and stayed to hear from the board after they returned from the closed session. Many attendees were disappointed, however, when the board returned and President Kaiser announced that they were still considering their options and would continue to investigate the matter and make a decision at a later time.

About a week later, the board asked Gerry to resign. They told him that in exchange for resigning, the school would continue to pay his salary for the balance of the school year. Gerry did not want to resign. He loved teaching music. And in spite of the hostile climate at his school, Gerry loved teaching the students of Byron Center High School. He rejected their proposal.

As Gerry drove home from the November 20 board meeting, it dawned on him that his sexual orientation was going to be the subject of the late-night local news shows. He was about to be publicly outed. Gerry's thoughts drifted to Cory and Cathy Schaaf. Gerry met the Schaafs in 1986, when he taught their sons the tuba and baritone horn at Grand Haven Christian School. Both sons went on to play music in college. Over the years Gerry attended their music performances, and after Gerry began working at Bryon Center, the Schaafs attended Gerry's high school concerts. Gerry deeply valued his relationship with the Schaaf family. He had never discussed his sexual orientation with them and was anxious about their reaction.

When Gerry arrived home after the board meeting, he immediately explained his predicament to Randy, "I've got to call them before they see this on TV." Gerry picked up the telephone, took a deep breath, and made the call. When he hung up the phone, Randy asked Gerry how it went. Gerry smiled, "They already knew."

Shortly after this conversation, the Schaafs wrote a letter to Superintendent Philip Swainston and the Byron Center school board urging them to "allow Gerry to keep using his God-given abilities" in their school. They continued, "It would be a gross misjustice [sic] if he were to be dismissed....The man has wonderful musical talents and they should be shared with others."

As a result of the media's coverage of the November 20 board meeting, parents who never objected to Gerry continuing to teach their children heard for the first time the vitriol directed against Gerry. The day after the news coverage, some parents called the school to complain about the way Gerry was being treated.

Skilling met with Gerry the same day to discuss the ongoing controversy. Skilling told Gerry that while he did not "agree with his lifestyle," he would stay neutral and support him as a teacher if he continued to do a good job. Gerry told Skilling that he knew some of the gay students at the school and that maybe because of his experience, he could help them with their struggles. Skilling immediately told Gerry that he should not talk to any students about their sexuality.

After this meeting Skilling met with Superintendent Swainston and told him he was alarmed about Gerry's comments. They called their attorney who instructed them to tell Gerry that he could not talk to students about their sexuality and that those types of conversations must be done by qualified counselors only.

The following day, November 22, Skilling met again with Gerry and gave him a memorandum directing him not to counsel students about their sexuality or discuss his sexuality with his students. The memo stated in part:

> I need to advise you as your principal that you should never allow yourself to be involved in the counseling of students on their sexuality. Also, at no time should you be discussing your sexuality to students in your class. These restrictions apply not only at school but also anywhere else. Remember you are always the teacher whether you are at school or anyplace where our students are present....
>
> Gerry please be very careful on this issue. This is the concern of the parents who oppose your lifestyle. They feel you will be influencing their student or other students to either accept this lifestyle or to become gay themselves. I am telling you this for your own protection and for the protection of the district.

Gerry was upset and asked, "Does this apply to all teachers?"

Skilling said that it applies to all teachers regardless of their sexual orientation. Skilling told Gerry that he wrote the memorandum for his—Gerry's—protection. From a legal standpoint, however, the memo served the school's interest but not Gerry's.

That the district would give Gerry this type of memorandum was not surprising. If a parent complained about a conversation Gerry had with their child, the memo provides a layer of protection for the school from potential liability. More importantly however, if Gerry violated the directive, the written directive could be used at a later date as a piece of evidence supporting discipline, including termination.

What the school failed to do, however, was focus on the needs of its gay students. The teen years are extremely difficult for students struggling to come to terms with their sexuality, a process which is further complicated for those raised in a religiously conservative community. It was gut-wrenching for these students to witness the persecution of their teacher for being gay. It was especially important during that time for the school to reach out to LGBTQ+ students, directly. To do so, however, would have required the administration to openly acknowledge that they had LGBTQ+ students and that those students deserved to be treated with dignity, and to recognize that it was the role of the district to support the well-being and education of those students. They did not have the capacity or willingness to do so.

6

Don't You Quit

By removing students from my classroom, parents have used their children to "make a statement." They have disrupted, all but gutted, the music program that I have developed over the past three years at Byron Center. They have destroyed the teamwork I had created among members of the band and choir and cut off their children from the richness that music can provide their lives. They have denied their children the opportunity to learn from someone who is different from themselves, to broaden their circle of acquaintances, and to learn to live in harmonious diversity.

Gerry Crane

After the November 20 board meeting, more reporters started covering the story. One day, Gerry and his union representative were holding a private meeting in a classroom. As they walked out, a reporter waiting in the hallway approached Gerry, with her camera rolling. Both Gerry and his union representative said, "No comment," and walked to the principal's office.

Principal Skilling contacted the station and told them they were not allowed in the building. They could, however, set up outside of the school. During the weeks that followed, when students and staff left the building, they would be confronted by reporters eager to interview them. Skilling instructed the staff not to talk to the media or get publicly involved in the controversy.

Thousands of letters flooded the school. Over one hundred

were the result of a letter-writing campaign, where a group created seven versions of a postcard message, all containing Bible quotes or religious messages: (1) "Praying for you ... in your dealings with the homosexual teacher"; (2) God's word reminds us to protect our young people from "this kind of lifestyle"; (3) "When the foundations are being destroyed, what can the righteous do?"; (4) "A student is not above his teacher, but everyone who is fully trained will be like his teacher"; (5) "The wicked freely strut about when what is vile is honored among men"; (6) "Do you not know that the wicked will not inherit the Kingdom of God? Do not be deceived: neither the sexually immoral nor idolaters nor adulterers nor male prostitutes nor homosexual offenders"; and (7) "Do not lie with a man as one lies with a woman."

Church officials at the First Reformed Church of Byron Center, the ones who signed the letter that was given to Gerry at the parent-teacher conferences earlier that month, sent a letter to the board. After listing numerous passages from the Bible, they called for a Christ-like response to Gerry, as opposed to a lynch mob mentality, explaining that they had an obligation to approach Gerry and urge him to repent of his sins and change his life. They expressed concern about both Gerry's soul and the well-being of the community.

There were also hundreds of letters of support. Student Nicholas Smith, a member of the choir and the drum major for the band, wrote a letter describing Gerry as respectful, caring, honest, responsible, hard-working, and devoted. He wrote that the loss of Mr. Crane would cause problems for many students, while only a few parents and students would remain angry if Mr. Crane continued teaching at the school. Thirty students signed Nicholas's letter.

Another student wrote a letter directly to Gerry and sent it along with an original poem thanking him for his dedication and telling him that he had given her strength and courage. The letter also illustrated the nature of rumors which were being spread about Gerry. She wrote that she did not know what happened because she was not "there," but that she knew he would not hurt anyone and that what people are saying about him is wrong.

People who supported Gerry raised a variety of points. For example, some parents held moral objections to homosexuality, but expressed their view that this fact was not relevant to Gerry's work as a teacher. One parent wrote that terminating Gerry's employment would send the wrong message to our children "that those who are different should be driven from our community." The parent explained: "I can only feel sorry for the children of parents so insecure in the values they have given their children that they must prevent them from exposure to anything else.... Giving in to this kind of intolerance also promotes hatred and violence by forcing society to become increasingly divided by its differences."[45]

A Christian woman from Holland, a nearby city, pushed back on the notion that homosexuality is a sin. Referring to the "persecution and witch hunt" she stated that the school is sending the message that Christians are "intolerant, bigoted, judgmental, prejudiced, pushy, and hateful."

Gerry's performance as a teacher was often mentioned by supporters. One parent reported that Gerry not only taught his daughter music but helped her gain the confidence she lacked throughout her school years.

The foremost concern for some was how firing Gerry would affect gay students. A man who identified himself as a longtime member of P-FLAG, the national organization of parents, family, and friends of gay people, wrote: "If you have 500 students in your school, the chances are that 50 of them are gay. This is their time of life when they are just discovering what gay means. They need role models and Mr. Crane could be one for your system.

Being gay drives many young gays to suicide—and is most apt to happen when society is repressive of what is natural."[46]

Similarly, a woman who identified herself as a member of a local Christian Reformed church and a Calvin College graduate urged the board to consider the consequences their decision will have on gay students in the school, adding, "Yes, folks, there are gay kids in Byron Center." She continued: "Right now, they're watching and absorbing the messages. They're hearing from some people that no matter how hard they try, no matter how good they are, they will never be accepted by their families, their society, their God. They're hearing that it is impossible for a gay person to be a moral person. Do you see the hopelessness that this can lead to?"[47]

These people were correct. Gay teachers, staff, and students throughout the district were devastated. It was terrifying to witness their colleague be publicly shamed, ridiculed, and scrutinized because of his sexual orientation.

Parents also pointed out the hypocrisy of the moral outrage. For example, one couple who believed homosexuality was a sin posited that treating this type of "sinner" differently from other sinners who engage in adultery or who steal was problematic. They wrote that a couple of years earlier quite a few teachers had committed adultery. The parents asked, "Should we now go back and fire all of them?"[48]

One woman signed her letter, "Name withheld because our society is still too close-minded. A pastor's wife in a nearby community." She explained that her views had changed after her twenty-four-year-old daughter came out to her as being lesbian. She wrote, "I have seen much more damage done by heterosexual teachers, ministers, and others in influential positions who cannot control their sexual urges than by homosexuals."

Others directed their outrage at the parents who were fueling the campaign against Gerry. One married couple with young girls in the district stood up for "Mr. Crane's right to privacy," writing: "It is demoralizing to us that fellow residents, no matter what their concerns, become so caught up in their own ideology that they leave no room for any other point of view." They also warned the board not to allow a handful of people dictate their decision.[49] One problem however was that some of the school officials and board members wanted Gerry ousted.

The parents of one student homed in on the heart of the matter: "While some choose to view the issue from a religious perspective and make moral judgments, the public school system is not a proper venue to promote personal religious convictions. Since any barriers to Mr. Crane's ability to perform his job are not the result of his own conduct, but the reaction of others to the situation, we feel that no action should be taken against Mr. Crane in his position as music director."[50]

In addition to his work at the high school, Gerry also gave individual music lessons on his own time. The parents of some of these students sent supportive letters to the school board. These parents spoke to Gerry's character and professionalism, in addition to his talent as a teacher. One couple, however, sent a letter to Gerry informing him that their daughter would no longer be taking piano lessons from him. Gerry had taught their daughter for years. They appreciated Gerry's teaching and musical abilities and wrote that their daughter enjoys playing the piano. Their Christian faith should not be defined by music, which they described as "so called wholesome and 'neutral' pursuits." They added that they would have likely continued to have Gerry teach piano to their daughter had he expressed that he was "not content in the gay lifestyle."

Prior to the next board meeting, Skilling told the staff that students cannot speak to media during school hours. If reporters asked the staff questions, Skilling instructed them to say that it is inappropriate to talk about someone's personal life.

Approximately 150 people attended the December 4 board meeting, requiring the meeting to be moved from the school district building to the high school. The board followed the same process used at the previous meeting: they listened to individual public comments about Gerry in a closed session. During the wait, a large group of people congregated around a table where Rev. Gregory, of the Byron Center Bible Church, was circulating a petition for people to read and sign. The "Petition on Homosexuality in Our Schools" was written in Old English font and read: "We the undersigned residents of Byron Center, affirm that the personal choice to indulge in the perversion of homosexuality by a teacher will inevitably impact his ability to provide a proper moral example for the students we have placed under his instruction. Therefore, his performance as a teacher in our school is unacceptable."

About thirty people signed it. The following week, Rev. Gregory turned in a second copy with about twenty-five additional signatures. Skilling attended Rev. Gregory's church and likely shared the beliefs contained in this petition.

After a long deliberation, the board exited the conference room and returned to their table to continue the public portion of the meeting. The board, however, did not release any information about their deliberations. Instead the president announced the board would issue a pronouncement two weeks later at their December 18 meeting.

A contingent from Westminster Presbyterian, Gerry's church, attended the December 4 meeting to support Gerry. They witnessed the large number of people who were using their Christian beliefs to condemn Gerry. After the meeting, they gathered at their church to debrief and discuss what they should do. They decided to draft a statement to present to their governing body for discussion and approval. Later, Westminster issued a statement affirming Gerry's commitment ceremony and a letter calling the district's actions "an attack not only on the moral character of a Westminster member, but also upon every other homosexual teacher."

On December 6, the principal of Byron Center Middle School, where Gerry taught music part-time, told Gerry that he would no longer be allowed to teach there, effective immediately. Skilling described the change as a reassignment. However Gerry was not reassigned to teach another class; instead he was told to use the extra time for administrative duties. Gerry was told that the decision was made for the sake of the music program.

A local paper, the Byron Center edition of *The Grand Rapids Press*, also known as the *South Advance*, ran a regular feature posing a question to its readers and publishing some of the answers the following week, along with photographs of the respondents. The paper was delivered to residents, and copies were placed in local stores and restaurants. In the midst of this controversy, the paper posited the question of whether a person's "sexual preference" should be an employment issue in public schools.[51] This edition published over sixty responses, including those from residents, parents, and high school students. Most responses supported the employment rights of a gay teacher. It was distributed on December 7, a few days after the board meeting and the day of the school's annual holiday choir concert.

In light of the firestorm surrounding Gerry's sexual orientation, some were concerned that a rumored protest would ruin the concert. Others worried that the turnout would be low. When Gerry took center stage, however, he faced a full house. Gerry was known for producing excellent concerts, and he did not disappoint. The students were energized and proud to showcase their work, along with their teacher's talent.

Prior to the last song of the night, a couple of students, feeling the emotions of the evening, stepped forward and hugged their teacher. Gerry took a moment to compose himself before directing the last song, "Our Gift for You," which the students sang and interpreted with sign language. As the song ended, most of the audience rose to their feet and enthusiastically applauded. Senior choir student Joc Pennington, along with two other students, presented Mr. Crane with a bouquet of flowers and a sweatshirt. While the applause continued, Joe and the other students made their way to the microphone and waited.

"We want to thank you, Mr. Crane," the students said before taking turns reading a poem they had written for Gerry. When they read the final line—"Don't you quit"—most in the audience stood and clapped, although a smaller group remained seated and silent. As the performance ended, students, with tears streaming down their faces, walked over to Gerry to exchange hugs.

On December 11, the school board held a special meeting to further discuss Gerry's future. This working meeting was closed to the public. The following week Principal Skilling sent the high school department chairs and union president a memorandum about "keeping the calm amidst the storm." The principal wrote in part: "We need to understand that this is only the beginning of the struggle, and we need to keep focused on what we are all about and that is educating our youth. Therefore, I need your help in putting together a plan that will address potential student disruptions at school and at the band concert on Tuesday, December 19, 1995."

The principal's warning that "this is only the beginning of the struggle" was curious. A public school administrator would more typically frame this as a controversy—a heated issue involving opposing sides. The word "struggle" typically implies one side of an issue, such as "the struggle for civil rights" or "the struggle to preserve family values." The principal's choice of words was a subtle indicator that he placed himself on one side of the controversy.

On December 14, a group of students met in a school hallway to discuss what they could do to support their teacher. What should they do if he were fired? The principal found out about their meeting and talked to them. According to a report written by Skilling, he told the students not to demonstrate or do anything "to disrupt the educational process" but that they could speak to the board, write a petition, or talk to the media.

On more than one occasion, Skilling told Gerry that he was acting as a neutral administrator. His actions, however, said otherwise. On the day of the December 18 board meeting, Skilling called a student out of her class to talk to her about Gerry. Skilling told the student, who was in the marching band, that her active support of Mr. Crane made her a "sinner, just like him." In spite of the principal's improper, unconstitutional attempt to browbeat her into submission, the student stood fast in her beliefs. Skilling told another student who had spoken out on Gerry's behalf that she might "fit in" better at an alternative school.

In December, a woman who was related to Gerry through marriage called Skilling and launched into a malicious rant against Gerry. She told the principal her opinion about Gerry's sexual orientation and about family matters, which included inaccurate statements, and none of which related to his work as a teacher or anything connected to the school. She gave the principal contact information but insisted that her name never be disclosed. Ignoring both the fact that her statements were irrelevant to Gerry's employment and the woman's request to not disclose her name, Skilling later attempted to use the statements against Gerry. He also divulged her name.

The Byron Center Education Association (BCEA), the local teacher's union, had 129 active members, one-third of whom worked at the high school. On December 13, the BCEA met to consider a motion supporting Gerry's right to continue teaching. When the meeting began, Gerry spoke to his colleagues from a prepared statement:

> I regret the difficulty of this situation. Thank you for your time in this busy season. Before coming to Byron Center, I taught at Grand Haven Christian, West Side Christian, and Wyoming Public Schools.
>
> I assure you that I did not bring any information about my life into the classroom. Nothing came from me. I have not engaged in any form of misconduct. I am not here to recruit. This is an educational institution and there is research to discredit that myth.
>
> It is my desire to remain teaching here and continue to serve this district and community. I am seeking a statement of unified support from this group of people. I believe my personal life should be private and so should yours.

Gerry listened as his colleagues discussed him and the related issues.

"We are deluding ourselves if we believe our private lives don't affect our teaching. We are public servants," said one teacher.

Another teacher countered this notion saying, "Our personal lives are ours. Who's next? How many of you have stuff in your personal life that you could be fired for?"

"No one has made more attempts to keep this out of the classroom than Gerry," another added.

Tom Hooker, a health and science teacher at the high school, referred to an article written by Rev. Gregory and argued that teachers cannot separate the personal from the professional and that they influence their students. Hooker said he would support Gerry if Gerry would reject his lifestyle. Hooker had been active in the campaign against Gerry's continued employment: he had signed the petition Rev. Gregory circulated; he had written a letter to the school board; and he had talked in closed session with the board. If the motion to support Gerry was passed, Hooker continued, then the opposing views should also be made public. He suggested that they issue a press release stating that those who did not support the motion are discouraged and saddened by it. Another high school teacher said, "We're fighting for the rights of a human being."

After continued discussion, the BCEA ultimately approved and issued a statement of support for Gerry. The vote was eighty-three members supporting the statement and twenty-five opposed. The statement read in part: "During the last three years, Mr. Crane has demonstrated that he is an exemplary teacher. Mr. Crane did not bring his private life into his teaching; it is unfortunate that it has become a public issue. The personal and private lives of teachers should not become public issues.... [Mr. Crane should] be afforded all rights due him under law and contract."

Members then considered a second motion to issue a press release containing the statement. The second motion passed with seventy-two members voting "yes" and thirty-one voting "no."

For Gerry, amid months of turmoil and public attack, this BCEA statement, issued on December 13, was good news.

The BCEA, however, did not specifically declare that Gerry's sexual orientation was irrelevant. Both Gerry and the BCEA side-stepped that definitive question, instead answering a broad question—and the question framed by Gerry—about whether the private lives of teachers should be made public. Gerry did not use the words "gay," "homosexuality," or "sexual orientation" in his statement to the BCEA. This decision probably reflected both Gerry's preference to not have his colleagues debate his sexual orientation, and the realities of the religious and political climate of the community, including his colleagues. For these reasons, Gerry's strategy made sense.

Yet how could one gay teacher survive this public vilification if a majority of his colleagues were not willing to specifically declare that his sexual orientation was irrelevant to his job? What stopped the BCEA from issuing a statement regarding the relevance of their colleague's sexual orientation? In part, it was the religious beliefs of many members. There were teachers who believed Gerry's sexual orientation was immoral, but they could support a generic statement about keeping teachers' personal lives private and affording him due process. In part, it was a crisis of courage. To issue a statement affirming a gay teacher's right to teach might have subjected BCEA members to some fraction of the harassment, ridicule, and publicity Gerry was himself experiencing. Regardless of the reason, the timidity of the statement meant Gerry would weather this storm alone.

At least one teacher at Byron Center wrote a letter to the board, telling them that it would be a terrible loss for the school and the students if Gerry left or was fired. Joanna Craik, a music teacher in the district, spoke to the growth in numbers—from a small group of students in choir and band to a select vocal group, two other large choirs, and a marching band—and to the quality of the music program. She explained that Gerry selects a "challenging and instructional repertoire" for his students, who now play at competitions and perform several times per year. She wrote that it would be extremely difficult to find a teacher who could do half as much, adding, "He is, in my mind, one in a million."

A couple of days after the BCEA's statement was issued, the

executive board of the county-wide teachers union—the Kent County Education Association (KCEA)—voted unanimously to support Gerry in his struggle for "fairness, decency, and justice."[52]

That same week, Skilling sent a memorandum to the faculty regarding, "Student and Outside Disturbances." The memo was from both Skilling and David Prindle, Gerry's union representative and president of the BCEA. The school was preparing for potential student, media, and outside disturbances, and had hired security guards for the December 18 board meeting and school day, and for the band concert the next day. The memo instructed teachers to monitor hallways between classes and to not discuss their opinions with students or allow class time to be used to discuss the board's actions. Students would not be allowed to protest, disrupt school, or wear clothing that either supported or opposed Gerry.

⌒

During the weekend Gerry and Randy found a reason to laugh. The Network had sponsored a night of comedy featuring Suzanne Westenhoefer, a lesbian comedian. When the show began, Network President Mary Banghart Therrien greeted the crowd and invited Gerry to the stage. He said a few words and the audience responded with heartfelt applause. Westenhoefer began her performance with a reference to Byron Center: "You're kidding. The music teacher is gay?"

⌒

Two days later, Gerry faced a different audience. On the day of the final board meeting of the year, December 18, Gerry was preparing students for their holiday band concert, scheduled for the next day. This created a complication for the trustees. One mother, whose daughter was starting college the following year as a music major, expressed her concern that her daughter's musical development would be hurt if Mr. Crane had to leave in the middle of the school year. She pointed out that the band's Christmas concert was scheduled for the day after their next school board meeting. She expressed concern for the band students if the concert was cancelled or interrupted.

December 18 was a stressful day for the music students. The school board had made it clear—they would be announcing their decision about their teacher that evening. What was going to happen to Mr. Crane? What would happen to their music classes?

Tammy Lee, a junior, was one of students who had an additional stake in the meeting. She had come out to herself in eighth or ninth grade.[53] During the fall of 1995 she was slowly starting to come out to others. Tammy was appalled that parents were pulling their children out of Gerry's classes. In a show of support, she dropped one of her classes, adding choir in its place. Tammy had attended all the board meetings about Gerry. As she was walking out of one of the meetings with a friend, Tammy felt empowered.

She turned to her classmate and said, "I have to tell you something."

"What?" her friend asked.

"I'm gay," Tammy said.

"You are?" her friend replied enthusiastically.

At the first three meetings, the trustees had remained silent. They listened to people in closed session and ended each meeting asserting they were still investigating the situation. Yet there was nothing to investigate. Gerry was outed as being gay, a fact he had not denied. The board had sufficient information to make a statement at their first meeting in November. Their delays fueled further outrage and created a basis for ongoing media coverage.

At the end of the December 18 meeting, after the board had met in closed session for ninety minutes, Kaiser, the president, stood in front of a packed gym and read its unanimous statement, which said in part:

> The Board wishes first to make it clear that it does not support or condone, in any manner, homosexuality as an alternative lifestyle. The Board firmly believes that homosexuality violates the dominant moral standard of the district's community. Individuals who espouse homosexuality do not constitute proper role models as teachers for students in this district.

After audience members hissed at this, he continued reading the statement:

> The Board takes its responsibility to the students and to the community very seriously. Within the constraints of the law, the Board will take all appropriate action to protect the students of this district from immoral conduct or the encouragement or condonation of immoral conduct.

> The district continues to investigate and monitor the current circumstance and controversy and will take prompt and appropriate lawful action when justified.

People in attendance were unclear what this carefully worded statement meant exactly. Kaiser read the last part of the statement again. For some, the confusion carried into the next day.

The next morning, the principal met with staff to discuss how they would handle the school day. In a report describing his instructions, Skilling wrote,

I told the staff they were not to wear buttons or ribbons in support of Mr. Crane because then the staff members who do not support Mr. Crane could wear them. We do not want to polarize our faculty. We need to stay neutral. I told the teachers that I was going to stay neutral as well. If we do not stay neutral this could cause a confrontation and could disrupt the education environment. I reminded them that we were here to be educators and that is where our focus should be. Our students have a right to an education.

Despite Skilling's directions at least three teachers had publicly opposed Gerry at the board meeting. Another employee sent a letter to other schools in the district containing the false claim that gay people "recruit" children.

After the staff meeting, when classes began, Skilling read a statement to the students explaining the school board's statement. He told them that the board had not discharged Mr. Crane. Skilling added that media reports saying a student was dismissed for supporting Mr. Crane were false. That evening Gerry directed the band in another successful performance to a packed house.

What was the meaning of the board's statement? Its use of the word "espouse," which means to support a belief or policy, was particularly problematic.[54] The import of the statement is that all teachers, staff, administrators—gay or straight—who support gay people, their rights, or causes are not proper role models for students. This pronouncement runs afoul of an employee's constitutional right to engage in free speech and association. Free speech includes the right to wear a T-shirt or baseball cap with the name of a gay non-profit organization, the right to place a gay pride bumper sticker on a car, and the right talk or write about supporting equality for gay people. The freedom of association includes attending a support group meeting for gay youth, attending a gay pride event, giving money to join a gay organization, or attending a gay couple's commitment ceremony.

In fact, the school board did attempt to dampen the free speech rights of another teacher during this time. One employee wore a button displaying the phrase "Welcome to Salem" to the December 18 board meeting. She was later told that the president of the school board expressed displeasure about her button to one of her colleagues. The employee wrote a letter to the president explaining:

> In 1692, hysteria reigned in Salem, Massachusetts stemming from behavior that the clergy of the town did not understand or condone. Twenty people were put to death and hundreds were accused, jailed, and ostracized.... I see a similar hysteria emerging in Byron Center. I see a fear of the unknown, and I am reminded of Salem, where innocent people were dealt with harshly and paid a heavy price for other's ignorance.[55]

She pointed out that her method of communication was not different from those who expressed their beliefs with signs, chants, literature, or press releases. By wearing a button containing the phrase "Welcome to Salem" at a school board meeting, the teacher spoke as a private citizen about a topic of public concern. The teacher's decision to wear the button did not prevent the district from operating in an efficient, disruption-free manner, which was the legal standard at the time.[56]

A remaining legal question, however, is whether the district applied its rules in a fair manner. In Gerry's case there were a handful of teachers who voiced their views that Gerry should not be teaching at the school because of his sexual orientation.

Did the board president express displeasure when they spoke out? If he did, it did not stop their behavior.

The school had evidence about Gerry's sexuality since mid-October. Based on the board's statement, therefore, they should have fired Gerry for being, in their opinion, an improper role model. Their decision not to fire him at that time may have been because they knew that terminating his employment would violate teacher tenure law. Teacher tenure is the legal right to continue employment unless the district has a reasonable cause for termination and has provided the teacher with due process. One important reason for tenure law is to prevent teachers from being subjected to the caprice of elected board officials who might make decisions to satisfy their personal motives or to appease the political whims of the day.

Gerry earned tenure in Byron Center during the summer of 1995. Under Michigan law in effect at the time, a tenured teacher could only be terminated for reasonable and just cause. The Byron Center teachers' contract addressed teachers' private lives as follows:

Article VII, Section B – Nondiscrimination and Private Life

Notwithstanding their employment, teachers shall be entitled to full rights of citizenship and no lawful religious or political activities of any teacher or the lack thereof shall be grounds for any discipline or discrimination with respect to the professional employment of such teacher unless detrimental to the United States. The private or personal life of any teacher is not within the appropriate concern or attention of the Board as long as the teacher in private life shall abstain from conduct which affects his relationship with students or the discharge of his/her teaching duties.

The board's statement that "individuals who espouse

homosexuality do not constitute proper role models as teachers for students in this district" violates the "Nondiscrimination and Private Life" protection in the contract. Being gay, attending a LGBTQ+ civil rights event, belonging to a church or religion that affirms the sexuality of everyone, participating in or attending a private commitment ceremony officiated by a minister—all of this is protected by a person's First Amendment rights to the freedoms of speech, association, and religion—and none of it negatively affects a teacher's relationship with students or their ability to discharge their teaching duties. Neither Gerry's contract nor the law gives parents the right to have their children taught by a teacher who shares their religious beliefs or political views.

One of the most difficult aspects of employment and constitutional law is to prove the employer's intent. Did the Byron Center school board have a discriminatory intent with their proclamation or were they attempting to address a legitimate, legal consideration? In this case, the board placed their motive in writing—homosexuals were bad role models for students. The reasonable inference of that public statement is that they wanted to rid their district of gay teachers. The board made no attempt to link their objection to Gerry to his performance as a teacher. Being gay was the problem.

Had Gerry decided to file a lawsuit, the board's statement would be the document his attorney would wave in front of the jury during closing argument while stating slowly and emphatically, "They did not want him to *be* gay."

Should Gerry have filed a lawsuit at that time against the school district for violating his constitutional rights? Not if he wanted to keep his job. Even if he wanted to file a lawsuit, Gerry's legal rights were limited—neither the federal government nor the state of Michigan prohibited LGBTQ+-based discrimination. Without an anti-discrimination law, Gerry was likely to lose a lawsuit.

He could have pursued legal action based on a violation of his freedom of speech, freedom of association, and due process. Yet filing a lawsuit based on the Constitution without a law prohibiting discrimination would require both Gerry and an attorney or national organization to be willing to be in litigation for years.

Gerry had been in contact with attorneys David Buckel and Patricia Logue at Lambda Legal. Founded in 1973, Lambda Legal is the oldest national legal advocacy organization for LGBTQ+ rights. It advocates for LGBTQ+ people, as well as people living with HIV. Legal organizations, such as Lambda Legal, decide whether to pursue litigation by examining the facts of the case and the law in the jurisdiction. Organizations seek what is referred to as an effective "test case" in an attempt to improve the likelihood of success. It is also referred to as "impact litigation." The selection of a test case involves consideration of the strength of the facts, the absence of facts which might distract the court from the main issue, other pending cases that are similar, and the political and legal leanings of a judge or jurisdiction. Gerry's exceptional performance reviews and the school board's December 18 statement would, at least regarding the facts, qualify as a potential test case. However, Gerry loved teaching music. He wanted to be known for being an excellent teacher, not a gay rights advocate.

The board's plan of action for 1996 was described in another part of their statement: "The district continues to investigate and monitor the current circumstance and controversy and will take prompt and appropriate lawful action when justified." Investigate and monitor what? The statement did not describe any teaching-related actions it planned to scrutinize.

The issue was that certain people inside and outside of the school district believed that homosexuality was a sin, that it was the type of sin that should prevent Gerry from teaching, and that their religious beliefs should carry the day in deciding who should be able to teach in a public school.

The board signaled their intent to keep Gerry's sexual orientation in the forefront. They put everyone on notice that they thought Gerry Crane should not be teaching in their district, but they were not prepared to fire him at that time. It infuriated those who believed Gerry's private life was irrelevant to his employment and were appalled that it had become a topic for public consumption. It emboldened those who wanted Gerry fired. For Gerry it meant that more was to come.

7

Inescapable

I had thought that, perhaps when the spotlight of the media atten-
tion dimmed, things might die down a bit. But, like fungus, bigotry
breeds and multiplies in its secret darkness.

Gerry Crane

Starting in mid-fall 1995, Gerry felt increasingly isolated from his colleagues at school. From all accounts they respected him as an educator, musician, and person of character. Yet at the board meetings, the only teachers and staff who spoke were those who were opposed to him continuing as a teacher. Teachers who wanted to actively support him were afraid to do so. Their concerns were valid. And if a gay teacher were to speak out, they risked being branded as an unacceptable role model like Gerry.

When Gerry was not teaching or interacting with students, his time at school was disheartening. He had regular interaction with his union representative, who attended meetings with Gerry, but this was union business. Entering and leaving the building, walking down hallways, and attending meetings was stressful. Gerry's presence seemed to trigger everyone's thoughts about the controversy. Some colleagues averted their eyes, or their smiles were more reserved.

When Gerry walked into the teachers' lounge, the cloud of controversy walked in with him. His presence reminded everyone of their relation to this problem, which triggered strong emotions. Teachers who attended local churches that were demanding that Gerry be fired shared that view. Some were uncomfortable having to even think or talk about homosexuality. Many grew weary of the media coverage and negative attention focused on their school. Their actions and expressions, however, did not necessarily reflect their feelings. A number of teachers were upset to witness how Gerry was being treated. Gerry limited his time in the teachers' lounge, typically eating alone in his office, which was located in the choir room. Eventually, students discovered he was spending his lunch period alone and began to join him. Gerry relished their support.

Randy was a crucial source of support for Gerry. He listened to and shared in Gerry's frustration and outrage. Randy felt the heartache that comes when watching a loved one suffer without being able to stop the source of the pain. Every day he witnessed the physical and emotional toll this was taking on Gerry. And while supporting his partner, Randy was harboring his own pain. After all, it was their commitment ceremony, their desire to formalize their union, that triggered this outpouring of hostility and hate. It was a public attack on their relationship.

For months the controversy seeped into their homelife, consuming their time together. The local newspaper, radio, and television often included the words *Byron Center, Gerry Crane, gay teacher,* and *homosexuality.* Any gap in new information was filled with letters to the editor, which were published a few times per week. *The Grand Rapids Press,* founded in 1893, later reported that this story garnered more letters than any other story in its history. Gerry and Randy could not simply ignore these reports. *Did the latest reports include new issues or accusations? Which parents*

*were writing letters? What did his students, their parents, and his
colleagues read or hear that evening? What could Gerry expect to
face at work the next day?*

Their mailbox and answering machine were primarily filled with
words of support and encouragement from friends, acquaintances,
and strangers. These nourished their sense of hope. The negative
letters were personal, preachy, and angry. Some wrote to warn
Gerry of *their* God's call for the death of homosexuals. Others
wrote to tell him that they were praying for him to change his
"lifestyle"—to save him from God's wrath. Together Gerry and
Randy shouldered the weight of the mail, messages, and media
coverage. They discussed their concerns, frustration, and options.

Gerry and Randy could not easily escape the controversy even
when they engaged in activities that used to be enjoyable. Gerry
was easily recognized by strangers because his photograph was
regularly in the news. If they ate at a local restaurant, someone
would walk over to talk to them. When they went to shop at the
mall, strangers would stare or point. When they saw friends and
supportive acquaintances in public, the conversations would be
about Byron Center. Byron Center became a constant intrusion
into their thoughts and daily life.

⌒

At Westminster, the church that had fortified their spiritual and
social life together, they continued to experience unconditional
love from Rev. Bill Evertsberg, Rev. Linda Knieriemen, and their
closest, treasured friends. They desperately needed to feel that love.

News coverage about Gerry often included references to Rev.
Evertsberg and their church, placing Westminster squarely within
the public controversy. Many Westminster congregants, along with
others in the community, were thrilled to see a local Christian

church acknowledge the humanity and worth of gay people. After hearing Gerry's story, many people started to attend the church. This was life-changing news for many gay Christians who were unaccustomed to finding support in a church.

The public attention was disconcerting, however, for those at Westminster who viewed homosexuality as a sin or who otherwise did not support gay unions. Many of these congregants were furious when they learned about Rev. Evertsberg's participation in Gerry and Randy's commitment ceremony. Friends of theirs would ask, "What's going on at your church?" in a disapproving tone. Many people left Westminster. While there was not a mass exodus, a continuous trickle of congregants leaving the church made clear the seriousness of the conflict. Some congregants who did not support their ministers' views chose to remain and voice their opposition. Rev. Evertsberg received scathing letters and comments from people both within and outside of the church. It was a turbulent time in the life of the church.

For Gerry, attending church was spiritually important, but he also felt the strain of his fellow congregants' disagreement. Gerry and Randy never wanted their commitment ceremony to cause problems; that was why they had decided to hold their ceremony at Meijer Gardens instead of in the church sanctuary. They felt bad that their minister—because he had officiated their ceremony—faced ongoing public attacks, not only by church members but also by the larger community.

Westminster is a part of the Presbyterian Church (USA) denomination, whose governing document is the Book of Order. In 1978 the church's General Assembly issued a "Policy Statement and Recommendations" regarding homosexuality, which stated that

Presbyterians should reject the sin of homosexuality in their own lives and challenge others to do the same, and that an unrepentant homosexual could not be ordained as a minister, elder, or deacon. The statement included three points that distinguished the denomination from many other Christian denominations: (1) Presbyterians should work to prevent society from continuing to hate, harass, and oppress homosexuals; (2) Presbyterians should work to decriminalize private homosexual acts between consenting adults and support laws that prohibit discrimination in employment, housing, and public accommodations based on sexual orientation; and (3) the church should continue to study and learn about homosexuality, emphasizing that "no opinion or decision is irreformable."[57]

On December 17, 1995, the governing board of Westminster church, consisting of approximately twenty people and referred to as "the Session," held a special meeting, which included Rev. Evertsberg and Rev. Knieriemen, to discuss Gerry's situation. After an hour of deliberation, the Session voted unanimously to prepare a written statement in support of Gerry to be sent to the church community. It read in full:

A Statement By The Session of Westminster Presbyterian Church Regarding Gerald Crane

With Gerald Crane's character at the center of a controversy in our community, the session (governing board) of Westminster Presbyterian Church would like the community to know that Mr. Crane is a loved and valued member of our congregation. We have benefited richly from his artistic excellence, collegiality, integrity, and grace.

Whereas others in the Kent County community are praying for Mr. Crane's conversion and redemption, we believe that Mr. Crane is made in the image of God, baptized into the covenant of faith, and already one of Christ's own. We affirm Mr. Crane's decision to enter into a lifelong covenant of commitment with his partner.

The Constitution of the Presbyterian Church (USA) commands its local congregations to be responsive to diversity in both the Church and the world: "Our unity in Christ enables and requires the Church to be open to all persons and to the varieties and talents and gifts of God's people ... providing for inclusiveness as a visible sign of the new humanity." We will continue to welcome Mr. Crane into the life of the congregation at Westminster Presbyterian Church, and hope that all people of goodwill are able to find a way to receive a blessing from his gifts.

This statement was sent to members of the church the day after Christmas, along with a cover letter, stating in part:

Most of you have been following the local media coverage of the controversy involving Mr. Gerald Crane, the Byron Center High School teacher whose tenured position fell into jeopardy when it was discovered that Mr. Crane is homosexual and involved in a covenant relationship with another man. Many of you perhaps do not know that Mr. Crane is a member of Westminster Presbyterian Church, as is his partner....

The session also recognizes that the Congregation will not share unanimity with the session, and that some Westminster members will disagree with the session's support of Mr. Crane. Indeed, the reality of same-sex covenanted relationships is a new issue for this session to be addressing, and each of the members find himself or herself in a different place as we work to understand this sensitive issue.

Nevertheless, the session reminds the congregation that the

Constitution of the Presbyterian Church (USA) states that "people of good conscience may differ." As part of its ongoing conversation, the session will be exploring ways for the congregation to have dialogue about this issue through the Adult Education program.

Some were pleased, but this did not end the controversy—there would be more to come.

⁓

It was 1996—a new year—and with it came a feeling of new beginnings. Gerry and Randy held hope that the controversy might diminish after the holidays.

Gerry returned to school after the break and was in his classroom getting ready for his choir class when students filed into the room and took their seats. Kim, a band student who was not in the choir class, walked in holding a drop slip and asked him to sign it. This was the standard procedure—students needed to talk to their teacher about the reason they wanted to leave the class and then obtain their approval. However in October 1995, Principal Skilling had instituted a new procedure that applied only to Gerry, which stated that students did not need to talk to him or obtain his signature. Kim's request was the first time since Gerry was outed that a student asked him to approve a drop request.

Before the holiday break, Kim had told Gerry that her church and her parents were pressuring her to drop band class. She had been in tears then. Now Gerry asked Kim whether her church was making her drop the class. He also asked if her church was pressuring her parents to make her drop the class. Kim replied "no" to both questions.

Gerry responded, "I'm not going to sign it now." He was preparing to teach choir.

Kim's parents complained to the principal about the way their daughter's drop request was handled. They felt that their daughter's classroom had become a political war zone and that the students were being used as pawns in the controversy. They also said that Kim expressed concerns after hearing that Gerry had played another student's instrument and that she was upset with the media coverage and students' opinions about Gerry. The administration took care of Kim's request to drop band class.

On January 16, Gerry was told that he had to meet with Skilling about a complaint. Vice Principal Noordeloos and Gerry's union representatives, David Prindle and Mike Stephens, were also at the meeting. Mike worked for the Michigan Education Association, and after the December 18 board meeting, he began attending some of the meetings. Skilling told Gerry that he was investigating a complaint about Kim's request to drop his class. Gerry explained the background of Kim's request: about the pressure from her church and her parents and that Kim had said before the holidays that she was told that her boyfriend might become gay from being in Gerry's class. Gerry said he told her that "no one becomes gay by being in my class" and that "only God makes you gay."

Gerry reminded Skilling that in October he had told Gerry that Gerry would no longer be approving requests to drop his classes. Gerry explained that Kim's request was the first one since the process was changed. Gerry also explained that on January 4 when Kim came into his class, he was getting ready to start his choir class. Gerry explained to the principal that he always tells his students not to bother him with peripheral things when he was getting ready to start class and that he didn't sign the drop slip because his class was starting and because he wanted to talk to Kim's parents first. He explained that since December he had tried to contact her parents by phone on three occasions.

Skilling acknowledged that he had changed the drop process in October, explaining that he instructed the school counselors not to use a drop slip when students were dropping Gerry's class due to his lifestyle. Skilling said that normally teachers and staff who sign a drop slip should ask the student the reason they want to drop the class but that it was inappropriate for Gerry to ask students about their religious beliefs or which church they attended. Gerry questioned why others could talk about their faith as a basis to condemn him, but he could not defend himself by talking about his. He also said that he believed he had an obligation to correct false information, such as the notion a person could become gay by taking a class with a gay teacher.

Gerry's comments to the principal need to be carefully unpacked. His position raises two questions. The first is whether a public school teacher should be able to correct false information—information, which in this case, was being used to assault Gerry's character. Gerry provided factual information when he told Kim that no one will become gay by being in his class. That is the type of statement that the school board and administrators should have made in the fall. It is accurate, however, that a student who is gay but closeted would feel affirmed by knowing that an adult whom they respect is also gay. This, in turn, could give the student the strength to come out. For some parents, this might be the rub—the presence of a publicly outed teacher would make it more likely that their children, or their children's friends, might come to better understand their own sexuality. These parents might recognize on some level that their child might be gay but prefer to live in denial, or hope that their child will be shamed into living in denial, or in their worst case scenario, that their child would pass as heterosexual by keeping most aspects of their life in the closet.

The second question raised by Gerry's comments is whether a public school teacher should be able to talk about his religious beliefs, given that others are using theirs to attack him. His comments raise First Amendment questions about the freedom of religion and the separation of church and state. The answer to this question depends on who Gerry is talking to about his beliefs. Gerry should not have asked the student questions about her church or share his belief that "God makes you gay."

It is not surprising that Gerry felt comfortable telling the student that "God makes you gay." It was natural for Gerry to frame important aspects of his life around his religious beliefs. Most of his educational experience as a student and a teacher, in both public and private schools, took place in environments where the belief in Christianity was accepted as the norm and promoted. Such a climate does not, however, make talk about God constitutional.

Byron Center was a public school that, to some extent, was run as if it were a Christian school. The school board meetings began with a Christian prayer; the health teacher read from the Bible during class; and a speaker, Rev. Peter Marshall, had been brought into the school to provide a Christian perspective of American history. In other words, Byron Center taught Bible-based curricula. The school not only promoted Christianity but also beliefs that were inconsistent with the teachings of many Christian denominations. And Gerry, the outed, gay, Presbyterian teacher, was held to a different standard than other teachers in the district.

Skilling investigated the complaint made by Kim's parents. As part of his investigation, he asked Kim if there were other students who witnessed her conversations with Gerry in December and on January 4. She gave the principal the names of three students. However, the principal talked to only one of these students. In his report, the principal wrote that he would speak to the other two witnesses "if needed," without explaining what would trigger that need. One of the students that he did not interview had spoken out publicly against the way the school was treating Gerry.

Principal Skilling also interviewed Brian Friddle, the school counselor. In his report, Skilling wrote: "I asked Mr. Friddle why [Kim] was going around with a drop slip if she was dropping for religious reasons? He said he did not know that was the reason. He said she must have picked up a drop slip in the office." Principal Skilling then called Kim and asked her how she had obtained the slip. She said that she started the drop process by going to the counselor's office and talking to Mr. Friddle, who asked her why she wanted to drop. She had explained that it was because of "the Crane thing."

In his report, Skilling continued: "I asked her if she was certain Mr. Friddle understood why she wanted to drop the class. [Kim] said[,] 'I think so but I am not certain.'"

On January 18, the principal gave Gerry two memoranda: a "written warning" for the conversation with Kim that took place in front of at least one other student (without stating that he did not interview two of the three witnesses) and for the way Gerry handled the student's request to drop the class on January 4, and a "written reprimand" for being insubordinate by discussing homosexuality with a student in the classroom on December 18, in violation of a November 22 directive that states, "You are never to discuss homosexuality or how you acquire it with students at any time."

Regarding the way Gerry handled Kim's drop request, the principal wrote, "It was unprofessional of you to show anger, pose those questions, and refuse to sign her drop slip." He concluded that Gerry had created a hostile environment for students based on their religious beliefs or convictions and wrote that for future requests Gerry should "promptly sign the form." The reprimand re-states the November directive: "You are never to discuss homosexuality or how you acquire it with students at any time."

Interestingly, neither memorandum stated that it was inappropriate for Gerry to talk about God in the classroom. At Byron Center the problem was not that a teacher shared his views about a Christian God—the problem was that those views weren't in sync with those of the dominant culture in town.

⌒

While the principal investigated Gerry, no one was investigating the principal. Counselor Friddle was not disciplined for violating the administration's procedure for handling student requests to drop Gerry's classes. The principal either believed the counselor's word over the student's or decided that the counselor should not be disciplined for telling the student that she needed to talk to Gerry and get his permission.

Gerry filed a grievance challenging the two disciplinary memoranda and seeking to have them removed from his file. As to the written warning, Gerry's position was that the discipline was unjustified because the student herself mentioned her church, stated (in December) she was being pressured, and stated that she was told her boyfriend could become gay by being in Gerry's class. Gerry said that he did not talk about religious beliefs or his personal life with her; instead he was explaining that a person cannot "catch" homosexuality from someone else. Gerry said he asked about her church in January based on what she had said in December when she had come to him in tears. Gerry also asserted that the administration had told him that they had established a special procedure to deal with student requests to drop his classes and that he would not be involved in that process; therefore it was actually the *counselor* who had violated the school's special policy by giving Kim a drop slip and telling her she needed to get his signature.

As to the written reprimand, Gerry said that he did not discuss his "lifestyle"; instead he was "correcting ignorance" by stating that a person cannot become gay by being in his class. Gerry asserted that a teacher's obligation to educate students includes a duty to correct false information.

The contract between the school district and Byron Center Education Association listed a five-step grievance process for teachers. The first two steps were to argue the merits of the grievance with the principal informally and then formally. Step three required the superintendent to approve or disapprove the grievance. Step four required the school board to review the grievance—through a hearing, an investigation, or another process—and then make a decision about the grievance. Step five required an impartial mediator to conduct binding arbitration.

Gerry's formal grievance was denied by the principal and superintendent. On March 18, the school board considered Gerry's grievance in closed session and supported the principal's decision. Next, Gerry requested binding arbitration, the fifth and final step of the grievance process. Arbitration was scheduled for May.

One day in February after Gerry had filed his grievance, the principal approached him at school and asked him to come into his office to talk. Gerry followed him into his office, and the principal told him the school was bringing Alan Keyes to speak to the students.

Alan Keyes, a Republican, was one of the most socially conservative candidates running for president that year. Keyes's platform was well-known. A self-proclaimed "family values" candidate, his touchstone issues were homosexuality, school prayer, and abortion. He believed that the concept of the separation of church and state was not supported by the Constitution. According to Keyes, the promotion of gay rights and abortion were the two major threats to our nation and that the intent of those who promoted gay rights was to destroy the family.

The principal told Gerry that he had talked to the superintendent about Keyes's family values platform and his opposition to homosexuality. Skilling explained that Keyes had originally been scheduled to speak at the high school on a school morning, but they had decided to move the rally to the Byron Center Community Center. It is unclear if the principal thought that Gerry would somehow be pleased to hear they made a decision to move the event to an off-site location in recognition of Keyes's anti-gay views. However, in reality, parents had complained about the Keyes event at the previous school board meeting.

"Will the students be required to attend this?" Gerry asked.

The principal said no. He added that the school had planned the event before Gerry's "issue" arose. Their intent, he asserted, was to educate students about government issues during an election year.

"So even government seniors will not be required to attend?" Gerry asked again.

The principal reiterated his answer—the students would not be required to attend.

"And you will make that clear to the students?" Gerry persisted.

Skilling said that they would make that clear.

"Are you going to provide a balance and allow for a Democratic position?" Gerry asked.

Skilling said that Carl Levin, the Democratic senator from Michigan, was going to be in town and that they were trying to schedule him for another event.

A few days later while Gerry was in the teachers' lounge, some of the teachers started talking about the Alan Keyes event, complaining that it was being "cancelled." Gerry felt that they were trying to get him to tell his opinion about the event, while also implying that it was *his* fault that the location was changed.

Gerry spoke up. "I think the students have a right to hear balanced views about political issues."

Others in the community were upset that the Keyes event was not going to be held in the high school. Some came to the next school board meeting to express their anger. They expected Keyes to talk about homosexuality, abortion, and the role of Christianity in public education. They wanted the students to hear these messages. From their perspective, moving the location would signal to the students that his message was somehow problematic.

On March 13, Keyes spoke to about four hundred students and adults. However, the event was *not* held at the community center but at a nearby Christian school, and the public school administrators arranged for their students to attend. Keyes told the students that America's survival depended on the nation's allegiance to God, specifically a Christian God. He said that American life will be destroyed unless people acknowledge that God exists.[58] Contrary to Skilling's assurances, some government class students were required to attend the event. The school never arranged for students to hear Senator Levin or any other Democratic candidate or officeholder.

On the same day that the local newspaper covered the Keyes event, it ran a story about harassment directed against Rev. Gregory, pastor of the Byron Center Bible Church. According to Rev. Gregory, the harassment started at the end of 1995, several days before Christmas, when he received in the mail a manila envelope containing the head of a bird, which he believed to be a quail or partridge; he reported this to the police. He also reported that during a Christmas Eve service at his church, a pungent odor of skunk spray permeated the church. Then, in February 1996, Rev. Gregory reported to the police that someone had recently sent him a blood-splattered note, which stated, "They are going to murder the bigot preacher and cut off his head like that bird on Foster Street," the location of Rev. Gregory's church. Gregory reported to the police that he and his wife were receiving about ten harassing phone calls per week and that the caller would often hang up after they answered the phone. At other times vulgar messages were left on their answering machine. These incidents were being investigated by the FBI and the Kent County Sheriff's Department.

Gerry and Randy had no hand in these events. They strongly opposed destroying property, threatening harm, and the mutilation of animals or any other type of violence. Gerry even opposed the use of peaceful protest against the school. He wanted administrators, his colleagues, and parents to stand up for one basic truth: that the character and effectiveness of a teacher is unrelated to their sexuality. Gay activist Phil Duran, a board member of The Network, stated that the organization did not participate in or condone these acts.

That the Keyes event and church harassment were covered by the news on the same day provides a window into Gerry's life. The school's inappropriate decision to require students to attend Keyes's talk, especially in the midst of Gerry's struggle to maintain his reputation and his employment, publicly connected Gerry's name to an anti-gay presidential candidate's campaign event. Similarly, the gruesome image of the dead bird, and the related harassment, could not be reported without using Gerry's name to place the acts in context. Few people, including public officials and celebrities, have their name connected to two different news articles of the day.

On Sunday, February 25, five days after Gerry was called into the office to talk about the Keyes event, he received even more disturbing news. He was told that hundreds of parishioners in Byron Center at many different churches had found a flyer tucked under the windshield wiper of their car after services that day. The flyer was a letter about "Mr. Crane, the Sodomite Music teacher"; it harshly criticized the school board for not firing Gerry and warned that the board opened the door "for more Sodomites to become teachers and to come out of the closet and be open about their moral perverseness." The letter, which was filled with Bible quotes, posited the question, "If the word of God demands the execution of these people, is it too much to demand that this man gets fired from his job as a teacher at Byron Center High School?"

Gerry was horrified. He and gay people throughout the community knew that after the church community was flooded with the message that "God demands the execution of these people," it may not take long for someone to carry out that demand.

Once more, Gerry had to summon the strength the next day to drive himself to school and walk into the building, knowing that the talk in the homes of many of his students the day before had been about him, framed as "the Sodomite Music Teacher."

Each complaint or event relating to Gerry—board meetings, the withdrawal of students, the Peter Marshall event, parent complaints, the Alan Keyes event, the flyer calling him a sodomite teacher—was accompanied by weeks of upheaval and harassment, including requests for interviews, more news coverage, parent and community complaints, questions to answer, responses to write, and always more meetings. Every meeting called by the principal required Gerry to call or meet with his local union rep, his state union rep, and his attorney. And it certainly required time to discuss it with Randy.

Gerry was exhausted.

1. Randy and Gerry, 1995.

2. The Apartment, Grand Rapids, Michigan.

3. Westminster Presbyterian Church,
Grand Rapids, Michigan.

4. School gymnasium bleachers during the December 18, 1995, school board meeting.

5. Gerry is hugged by a student after the December 18, 1995, school board meeting.

6. Gerry directing the West Michigan Gay Community Chorus
during rehearsal, December 1996.

GERALD M. CRANE
August 25, 1964
to January 3, 1997

For the lessons that you taught us,
And the music that you made,
For the gentle love you brought us,
And the heavy price you paid.

For integrity and courage —
The examples that you set,
Though you're gone,
*   we aren't discouraged;*
Gerry Crane, we won't forget.

Paid for by members and supporters of

THE**NETWORK**
The Lesbian & Gay Community Network of Western Michigan, Inc.

Contributions can be made to The Gerald M. Crane Memorial Music Scholarship Fund c/o The Grand Rapids Foundation

7. From memorial page placed in *The Grand Rapids Press* by
The Lesbian and Gay Community Network, 1997.

8

Escalation

I have been accused of "promoting" homosexuality. I have been attacked for "choosing" an "alternative lifestyle." I have been formally reprimanded for doing what a teacher does—attempting to educate with facts those individuals who attack with opinion based on interpretation.

Gerry Crane

Things felt good. Two consecutive days at school were calm. No harassment. No unfounded accusations. Gerry soaked it in.

At home after the second day of reprieve, Gerry received a telephone call from a student, followed quickly by calls from other students and parents. They had all come home to mailboxes filled with anti-gay propaganda. Each family had received a package containing a video, a book, and a letter signed by approximately forty members of a group called Parents for Traditional Values. The signatories included people from Rev. Gregory's church, Byron Center Bible Church, and Resurrection Life Church. The letter referred to "the tremendous moral storms that are sweeping our country" and urged parents to read and view the enclosed materials "to better understand what the gay lifestyle means." Although the letter did not mention Gerry's name, the message was clear.

The forty-minute video, *Gay Rights, Special Rights*, was produced by Jeremiah Films.[59] It features clips from the 1993 March on Washington for Lesbian, Gay, and Bi Equal Rights and Liberation, interspersed with commentary from leaders of the national anti-gay movement, such as Rev. Lou Sheldon, chairman of the Traditional Values Coalition; Ralph Reed, executive director of the Christian Coalition; Trent Lott, Republican senator from Mississippi; and William Bennett, former Secretary of Education during the Reagan Administration. The anti-gay speakers also included Rev. Peter Marshall, the speaker at the student assembly in November 1995, and Joseph Nicolosi, the author associated with the conversion therapy support group Hypernican, which Gerry and Bruce Klein-Wassink had previously attended.

The images in the film include gay people kissing, holding hands, dancing, and people dressed in drag, leather, and sexually revealing outfits. The clips show people holding banners and signs with messages such as, "Keep Your Church Out of My Crotch," "Fuck the church, Fuck the state, Hormones will decide my fate," "I'm Gay and I Teach America's Children," and "We're here, we're gay, we're in the PTA." The anti-gay speakers warn about the "dark realities entrenched in the homosexual lifestyle" and the "behavior disorder that goes along with homosexuality" and caution viewers that "the media does not tell us anything about the abhorrent lifestyle of these people." The voice-over includes detailed descriptions of sexual acts—with the implication that only homosexuals engage in these practices.

During a clip of a drag show, the voice-over states, "Our children are going to be the losers." The video shows a close-up of a toddler crying, and the camera slowly zooms out to reveal that the boy is being held by a man. As the boy continues to cry, another voice-over instructs viewers to be vigilant: "Young boys are so vulnerable. They are at an age where they like boys, and homosexuals will say, 'Of course you don't like girls; you're one of us.' This is a serious, serious matter. People don't realize we are going to lose thousands, thousands, and thousands of good heterosexuals."

Another voice-over repeats a portion of a provocative essay written by a gay author: "We shall sodomize your sons, emblems of your feeble masculinity, of your shallow dreams and vulgar lies. We shall seduce them in your schools, in your dormitories, in your gymnasiums, in your locker rooms." The essay, written in 1987 by Michael Swift, was initially published in the *Gay Community News* in Boston. The voice-over did not include the first sentence of the essay, which provides its intent: "This essay is an outré, madness, a tragic, cruel fantasy, an eruption of inner rage, on how the oppressed desperately dream of being the oppressor." The religious right has referred to this essay as "The Homosexual Manifesto" and has cited it for many years *without* the introductory sentence. The film ends by informing viewers that they can obtain an action packet by contacting the Traditional Values Coalition in Anaheim, California.

The package sent to parents also contained the book *Behind The Headlines, Setting the Record Straight: What Research Really Says About the Social Consequences of Homosexuality*, published in 1994 by Focus on the Family and written by Larry Burtoft, Senior Fellow for Family, Church and Society Studies at Focus on the Family Institute. The theme of the 150-page book is that homosexuals are immoral people who threaten the family, children, public health, and society at large. It describes the "dark shadow" of homosexuality and its negative effects "upon the natural family and its most valuable fruit, children."

Early in the book, Burtoft answers the question, "What do homosexuals do?" with a bulleted list of explicit sexual acts: mutual masturbation, oral copulation, anal copulation, anal/oral sex, and vaginal/oral sex. The author further asserts that a minority of homosexuals also engage in anal/manual sex, sadomasochism, urinal sex, pedophilia, and group sex. Each term is followed with an explicit description of the sexual act. The book states that pedophilia "runs high among male homosexuals who have embraced the philosophical underpinnings of the gay agenda." Anti-gay organizations have historically and consistently conflated being gay with pedophilia. The messages are: be afraid, gay men will rape your boys, it is in their nature, it is the essence of being gay. These spurious claims are not supported by statistics and social science research.

⌒‿⌐

The day after learning about the mailing, Gerry had to summon the energy to go to school, face his colleagues, and stand in front of a room of students each hour and teach music, while wondering: Did the students watch the video? Did they read the book? What did their parents say to them? What was the talk among students?

Students *were* talking about the mailing. Gerry didn't ask students about it, but many told him what they thought. One student said, "They're just trying to make us hate you."

At the basketball game the next day, the bleacher talk was all about the propaganda package. Adults and students shared information, insights, and questions. Were school administrators involved? Were teachers involved? How did the sender get everyone's name and mailing address? By the end of the game, some students surmised that a school employee sent the material. James Morin, a sophomore in the band, said that his last name on the mailing label was misspelled in the same way as on other mail sent from the school.

Some parents would not let their children watch the video or read the book, while at least a few of them immediately threw out the materials. However, others watched the video and were fine with having their children view it. One group of students gathered for a party to watch the video together. Interestingly, there were a few families that did not receive the mailing, including Jim and

Kathy Jauw, whose two children played in the band, who had vocally and consistently supported Gerry.

The families received the mailing the day before parent-teacher conferences. As they each took their turn to sit down with Gerry, the fact and content of this mailing permeated the air around them. Gerry wondered if they were blaming him because their school and town had become a spectacle. What were they thinking about when he needed to tell them concerns or problems about their child? Were they imagining Gerry as one of the men at the gay pride march, scantily clad in leather? Were they thinking about the sexual acts described in the book and film? If he spoke of their child in glowing terms—would they think about the connection the book made between homosexuality and pedophilia? Were they angry because they had to think about his sexual orientation instead of thinking about what he had to say about their child's school work? When, if ever, would the public humiliation stop?

After conferences ended that night, Gerry thought about the parents who told him they were upset that the material was sent to them. Gerry wondered if they were mad enough to do something about it.

The mailing was discussed at the March 4 school board meeting, meaning in effect that Gerry's sexual orientation was again the subject of a public meeting covered by the media. Members of Parents for Traditional Values voiced their view that the video accurately depicted the homosexual lifestyle. Their intent was not to attack Gerry, they asserted, but to protect their children from the immorality of homosexuality.

Parents who were upset that their personal contact information was released called for an investigation into how the group obtained the mailing list. Those who supported Gerry thought that the school needed to stop talking about homosexuality and move on. Gerry was being unfairly attacked and none of this was good for the students. They wanted administrators to let Gerry focus on his teaching.

For the members of Parents for Traditional Values, the video and book evidenced the evils of homosexuality and was intended to convince others to join their crusade against Gerry. What they did not know, however, was that the video became a lifeline for at least some of the gay students at the school. When the video arrived at Tammy Lee's house, she popped it into the VCR, not knowing what to expect. Seen through the eyes of a teen growing up in Byron Center, who was in the midst of her own coming-out journey, the video was empowering—Tammy saw thousands of people of all stripes openly expressing their sexual orientation and gender identity through their dress, comradery, love, music, dance, and activism. The film made Tammy realize she was not alone. In 1996, she did not have the benefit of growing up in a culture filled with gay role models. The internet was less developed and social media did not exist. Like most teenagers at the time, she came of age without knowing about the strong, affirming gay communities in larger cities, and even in Grand Rapids.

Charlie Comero, a tenth-grade choir student who had come out during the prior year, also watched the video after school that day and initially thought "this is sweet." Similar to Tammy's reaction, Charlie found it exhilarating to see so many gay and transgender people celebrating together. After continuing to watch the film however, Charlie became disgusted with the way the filmmakers manipulated the footage to create anti-gay propaganda and furious that this was being used incite hate and ridicule in their school. Charlie removed the video, took it outside and burned it.

Tammy and Charlie were further along in understanding their own identity than most of their classmates who came out at a later time in their lives. For all of these students the video solidified stereotypes and roused feelings of despair.

The school conducted an investigation to determine if any school officials played an inappropriate role in the mailing. As part of this investigation, Gerry, *the target of the mailing*, was called to the district building to be interrogated by the school's attorney in Superintendent Swainston's office. The attorney, Pat White, said he was trying to determine if the school had been inappropriately involved in providing names and addresses for the mailing.

"Do you have mailing lists with student names and addresses?" White asked Gerry.

"Why are you asking *me*? You're asking the wrong person," Gerry responded.

"We just need to know," the attorney said.

Gerry said he had a mailing list of the students who attended band camp but did not have the addresses for his choir students. The attorney questioned Gerry about how often he used the list.

White said the district's Personnel Committee wanted to know if he ever used the students' instruments for demonstrations and if he had separate mouthpieces for each instrument. The attorney stated that there were some recent studies about saliva transmitting the AIDS virus.

Upon hearing this question, Gerry stood up. "This conversation is over. I am not answering anything until I talk to counsel."

The attorney persisted with questions and eventually requested the names and telephone numbers of the band boosters. Gerry again stated he would not provide this information until he talked to his attorney. White told Gerry that they suspended the last person who refused to answer their questions.

"I'm not saying or offering anything until I seek counsel," Gerry repeated.

Later that day, after speaking to his attorney, Gerry gathered the information the attorney had requested and submitted it. Gerry also informed White that at times he brought his own trumpet and clarinet to school and that there were other times when he played a student's instrument.

White also interviewed school counselor, Brian Friddle, to determine if he was involved with the mailing. Friddle initially said that he did not know anything about it. Later, however, Friddle admitted that he knew that Ron Reisterer, the director of technology for the high school, was generating a copy of the student address list and that it was going to be used for the mailing.

The school concluded that Reisterer had used his access to the student database to obtain the addresses. Reisterer eventually acknowledged his involvement and admitted he knew the reason why the group Parents for Traditional Values wanted the addresses. Reisterer contended that his actions did not reflect his personal opinions about homosexuality. He described the group as an active, reliable organization, and he did not think he needed authorization to release the addresses to them since he released the data to other organizations, such as colleges, universities, the military, and companies that sell class rings, and caps and gowns.

On March 8, Superintendent Swainston informed Reisterer that he was recommending the board terminate his employment. The superintendent provided the board with three reasons for his decision, writing:

1. During the investigation of the possible inappropriate release of student names and addresses, Mr. Reisterer repeatedly lied to the Superintendent by denying any knowledge of, or participation in, the generation of a current list of student names and addresses which was provided to an outside citizen group. Further, he provided false information designed

to mislead regarding the nature and origin of the student information obtained by the private citizens group.

2. Mr. Reisterer, without authorization and in violation of District policies and the Federal Family Education and Privacy Rights Act, provided student names and addresses from the District's data base to a private citizens group.

3. Mr. Reisterer misused his access to the school's record data base to further his own personal agenda.

The superintendent emphasized that information in the databases is highly confidential and protected by state and federal law, and concluded that the person occupying the Director of Technology position: "must be absolutely trustworthy in not abusing this position and the access it provides. The students and public deserve no less.... I have lost all trust and confidence in Mr. Reisterer to faithfully and honestly perform the full range of his responsibilities to the District."

After sending Reisterer a copy of this recommendation, the superintendent provided him with the opportunity to resign prior to the special board meeting which was scheduled for the evening of March 11. Reisterer did not exercise this option. He placed the fate of his continued employment in the hands of the school board. During a closed-door meeting, the board voted to *reject* the superintendent's recommendation for termination and instead imposed only an unpaid, four-week suspension. Neither Gerry nor the public knew that the superintendent had recommended the board fire Reisterer.

Separately, the superintendent suspended Brian Friddle for two weeks without pay for initially providing false information to the school during their investigation. Superintendent Swainston sent Friddle a letter of discipline which documented the suspension and placed Friddle "under strict supervision." According to the letter,

Friddle would be required to maintain regular logs and attend weekly meetings for an unspecified period of time. The letter did not explain the content of the logs or the purpose of the meetings.

Astonishingly, only six days later, Assistant Superintendent Robert Wait wrote a memo to Friddle, and sent a copy of the letter to Superintendent Swainston, stating, "Congratulations! It is my pleasure to inform you that the Board of Education has approved your continued employment ... as a third-year probationary teacher for the 1996–1997 school year. We compliment you on successfully completing your second year of probation. We appreciate your outstanding efforts throughout this school year." Friddle's suspension ran from March 17 to March 30. This four sentence congratulatory letter, dated March 19, did not refer to his disciplinary suspension.

In spite of Superintendent Swainston's recommendation to the school board to fire Reisterer, on March 14 he issued a public statement, which said in part:

> The actions of the district employees did not violate official school policies which state that directory information "can be given to any person or organization for non-profit-making purposes when requested, unless the parents of the students restrict the information" at the time of the annual District notification. In the policies of the District, Directory information is differentiated from Confidential Records. No laws, state or federal, were violated.

> Mr. Ronald Reisterer and Mr. Brian Friddle are receiving suspensions without pay by the Board of Education for not initially cooperating in the investigation conducted by the School's attorney. In addition, the Board of Education has directed the superintendent to clarify the District's student record policy

and provide training for all current and future staff members on that policy.

Some thought this discipline was not enough. The names and addresses of parents were now permanently in the hands of both this local group and possibly regional and national organizations. Tax dollars were used to publicly target and humiliate a teacher. Their actions disrupted the educational environment, generated attorney fees for the district, and created additional media coverage of their school, damaging the school's already precarious reputation. All of which raises the question: Did these men act as proper role models for the students? The Superintendent's statement did not connect their actions in facilitating the mailing to the ongoing controversy about Gerry. Nor did it mention that Skilling directed teachers and staff to be neutral.

Some teachers and administrators believed that Reisterer and Friddle were being treated unfairly—that their reputations were unjustly attacked. In their eyes the problem was not the behavior of these two men. The problem was that an outed gay man taught in the school.

Skilling, Friddle, and Reisterer shared similar religious beliefs. All three attended Rev. Gregory's Byron Center Bible Church. Reisterer obtained undergraduate and graduate degrees from Liberty University, an evangelical, anti-gay university founded by Jerry Falwell.

Later, in 1998, an administrator described Reisterer as being "very loyal to our district." That same year, a recently promoted assistant superintendent wrote "a commitment was made to Ron by Bob Wait [the previous assistant superintendent] for 40 vacation days for the 1997–1998 school year.... I honored this commitment when I was hired as Assistant Superintendent but for this school year only." The memo does not explain the reason for the commitment or the date it was made. Reisterer's employment contract awarded him twenty-five days of vacation per year; therefore, the commitment from Wait gave Reisterer an additional three weeks of vacation. The memo also stated that after the 1998–1999 school year, his vacation period would return to twenty-five days. The vague nature of this commitment, coupled with Reisterer's suspension in 1996, raises a question: why would an assistant superintendent commit to giving an employee three additional weeks of vacation for only one school year?

As a result of the video mailing, media attention now focused on the improper actions of school employees who wanted Gerry fired. Headlines stated that school employees used student mailing lists for political and religious purposes. Skilling moved into damage control mode.

Skilling started asking people to write letters to the newspapers extolling commendable aspects of the school. He talked to a few students individually. At least two of those students felt pressured to write letters. One refused. Another wrote the type of letter her principal wanted and later regretted doing so. Skilling also asked Gerry's union rep, David Prindle, to write a letter to the local paper. This letter was published in Byron Center's local paper, the *Southern Advance*. "Even though our staff may have differing opinions we still are putting the students first," he wrote, followed by a list of the school's accomplishments, including praise for the music program and Best Band award.[60] Gerry's name was not mentioned.

By mid-March the staff had heard about the results of the school's investigation. During a meeting that week, some of the teachers expressed anger about the mailing. Principal Skilling, however, defended Friddle by implying that he had been courageous in coming forward after lying, adding that anyone can lie in a moment of weakness. Skilling also talked about how difficult it had become for staff to wear their Bulldogs gear in public because they were subjected to jokes and questions. A teacher, referring to the controversy, said, "This is not going to stop. It's hurt us all a lot." Gerry listened to his boss and colleagues discuss what had become publicly known as "the Gerry Crane controversy." He wrote his thoughts on paper, "I'm furious about how tolerant this staff has been toward this shit. Finally (I think) Shoe [his nickname for one of the teachers] and a few others are stirred."

The mailing was intended to exacerbate moral outrage. While some of the people responsible continued to insist that they were not attacking Gerry, the material falsely stated that gay men were more likely to be pedophiles. Gerry was the only out gay person in the school. They knew it would be humiliating. They knew it would be covered in the media.

It was another attempt to drive Gerry out. It was sent to provoke one of two outcomes—to enlist more parents to call for his dismissal or to compel Gerry to resign. To advance the second objective, in March, school officials again told Gerry they would provide him with severance pay if he would resign immediately.

Gerry was enraged. But he did not give in to the coercion. Instead, after the investigation concluded, Gerry made a formal complaint against Reisterer and Friddle based on three points: (1) they used their positions with the school to advance their personal religious beliefs; (2) they defamed Gerry's character; and (3) they violated school district policy by causing a disruption among staff in the school.

According to the school district's ethical standards, staff were prohibited from using their "position or public property for political or religious purposes." The district also limited staff's freedom of speech, prohibiting "personally defamatory comments about co-workers" and stating that staff "should refrain from making public expressions which are made without regard for truth or accuracy." Gerry wrote that Reisterer and Friddle used their school positions and property to further their personal political and religious purposes. He argued that they distributed defamatory anti-homosexual propaganda "to the homes of my students" that was "meant to cause direct conflict between myself, my students, and their families—all to advance their personal religious purposes. Additionally, the content of the mailing was one-sided, inflammatory, and degrading—all aimed at defaming my character and the character of the homosexual community at large." He ended his complaint by stating that proper discipline was needed to afford all employees the same rights and responsibilities so that everyone "will be held accountable to the same professional and ethical standard that this community claims to uphold." Gerry sent a copy of this complaint to Superintendent Swainston, Assistant Superintendent Robert Wait, and his union representative, Dave Prindle.

The principal trivialized Gerry's complaint. During separate conversations with Friddle and Reisterer, he told them that he did not think much would come of it. Skilling met with Gerry on April 12. He asked Gerry why he thought Friddle and Reisterer should receive additional discipline. Gerry responded, "Because they used their school position to advance [their] personal religious beliefs and defame my character." Gerry added, "They were never punished for this to begin with. It was a smoke screen for not cooperating with Pat White." Skilling later wrote, "Gerry was agitated when I asked this question. I do not think he likes you Pat [referring to Pat White] I hope you are not offended."

As Principal Skilling predicted, or more accurately, consistent with the way he orchestrated the investigation, nothing came of Gerry's complaint.

Was it time for Gerry to leave? Would more people step up to support him? Would their support make a difference?

9

Time

Unless the law mandates, Byron Center School District's Board and parents clearly will not accept diversity in their schools. Unless the law commands, Byron Center students will not be raised to accept the consequences of their own behavior; instead, they will be taught to find others to blame. Unless the law protects, Byron Center administrators will, in their own words, "continue to investigate and monitor" my life both inside and outside the classroom.

Gerry Crane

Those who loved Gerry, both his gay and straight friends, were furious watching people at his school and in the community publicly eviscerate him. They knew that the relentless attacks took a heavy toll on him, and they saw the cumulative effect on his emotional and physical health. While they surrounded him with love and support, they recognized that they could not shield him from the accusations or the isolation he felt within the walls of his school.

Those in the local gay community who didn't know Gerry personally were also pained. While they were not surprised that many people voiced their anti-gay beliefs, they did feel overwhelmed hearing the venom on a regular basis and observing the lengths people went to publicly destroy the reputation and career of a gifted and devoted teacher.

And there was no relief in sight.

A growing number of people in the gay community wanted to

do more than attend board meetings and write letters; they wanted to engage in public, organized advocacy on behalf of Gerry.

One Sunday afternoon, a group of friends, supporters, and local activists met at Gerry and Randy's house to discuss options. As a member of The Network board and a local activist, I also attended this meeting.

Gerry greeted people at the door, extended a hand or embrace, and thanked each person for coming. The warmth in his eyes and sincerity in his voice contrasted with his slightly agitated movements. Gerry was by nature a private person. Yet he found himself welcoming into his home a group of people who came with the express intent to discuss the status and future of his employment. Over the course of a few months, Gerry had become a public person, recognized not for his work as a music teacher but instead as a victim of discrimination and an object of disdain and ridicule.

Some people in Gerry's living room that afternoon engaged in public activism. Gerry valued their support. Yet what he yearned for was that the adults who witnessed his work—colleagues, administrators, and parents—would express their outrage and would support him as an effective music teacher who added great value to the educational and developmental lives of his students.

Appropriately, Gerry's polished, black baby grand piano was the anchoring object in his living room. As people arrived, they exchanged greetings with those they knew and extended introductions to others who were meeting for the first time. The crowd overflowed into his dining room.

Randy projected his deep voice over the chatter to signal the start of the meeting. Gerry thanked everyone for coming, and then gave a short update about matters at school. He paused, leaving others to begin the discussion. In short order, people started expressing their anger about how Gerry was being treated:

"How can they treat you like this?"

"It's a public school."

"They won't fire you because they don't want a lawsuit."

"What do your lawyers say?"

"We need to get more people involved."

"The Bible-thumpers are getting all the media attention."

People shared anecdotes about other gay people, especially teachers, who were afraid to even join in conversations when the topic arose at their schools. They also discussed allies and groups who might get involved to support Gerry.

Then the telephone rang.

Randy went into the kitchen to answer it. He returned to summon Gerry to take the call. The discussion continued. After a few minutes, Gerry returned to the living room. He explained that the call was from an attorney, David Buckel, from Lambda Legal.

Gerry said in a weary voice, "They had some questions."

Gerry remained standing as others continued the conversation.

After listening to people express their anger and frustration, Jeff Swanson spoke up. Jeff and his partner, Dennis Komac, owned the gay coffeehouse Sons & Daughters. They had brought their outspoken brand of activism from California to Grand Rapids in the mid-1980s, and Jeff was instrumental in forming The Network in 1987.

A tall man, with a large frame and personality, Jeff declared, "We need to gather a large number of people, go to Byron Center, and protest outside that school every day."

Jeff's approach reflected the work of the gay liberation movement in the late 1960s and 1970s where protests were indispensable, and the work of AIDS activists in the 1980s where ACT-UP members engaged in creative, theatrical, provocative demonstrations using signs, costumes, and props.[61]

In 1996 in Byron Center, the religious right controlled the political stage and drowned out opposing views. They were successfully enflaming people's fears—parents' fear of having a gay man teach their children, officials' fear of being voted out of office, gay people's fear of being shunned in the community, employees' fear of being fired from jobs in education, and *some* Christians' fear of missing out on eternal life.

Jeff thought they should not continue to make nice with the school board and administrators in the vain hope that the school would respond to reason and decency. He believed the gay community and like-minded people needed to vocalize their opposition while developing and maintaining a large, sustained presence. It was time—no, it was long past the time—for the gay community to take their outrage to Byron Center. It was time to protest outside of the school.

While Jeff continued to make his case for public protest, the people in the room silently divided into two camps: those who were actively looking at and listening to Jeff and those who sat back with expressions of concern, looking at Gerry, Randy, and each other. When Jeff concluded, people quickly interjected, speaking over each other. Some expressed their willingness to protest: "I'll be there"; "Count me in"; "Tell me when and where." Others countered: "We don't want Gerry to lose his job"; "Protesting will make it worse"; "They won't care"; "We need to do what Gerry wants."

Slowly more people looked at Gerry.

Gerry, appearing worn and stressed, said he did not want protests at his school. He wanted school time to be about the students. And he didn't want to lose his job.

Someone suggested protesting at a different location. However support for that option waned quickly. People wanted to support and advocate for Gerry but not go against his wishes.

People had come to this meeting angry at Byron Center—the words "Byron Center" had come to encompass the school district, its board, administrators, attorneys, employees, and others in the community who were assailing their friend. Yet people had also come with hope that they could help. They wanted to leave with a plan of action. They wanted to hear that steps could be taken to stop the attacks. They didn't want to hear that they needed to wait and witness whatever happened next. This was a public school. There were people in west Michigan, including Christians, who understood the difference between a public school and a private religious school. Gerry had the support of Lambda Legal, the Michigan Education Association, the Human Rights Campaign, and the Gay, Lesbian & Straight Education Network (GLSEN).[62] Couldn't anyone do something to protect Gerry and his job?

The meeting started to wind down. As people left, Gerry thanked each person individually. But, as they walked to their cars and drove home, they felt dejected.

The local school board elections were scheduled for June 10. There were two open seats. In mid-April Marvin Schierbeek, one of the people who had called for Gerry's dismissal in the fall, announced that he was running. Announcing his candidacy, he said was committed to preserving the community's Christian heritage. His wife expressed her belief that Satan was making headway in their community. Another candidate, Dean Sullivan, had shared his views with Gerry in February. Sullivan had told Gerry that he had been praying for him. He heard that Gerry attended Cornerstone College, (previously Grand Rapids Baptist College) and told Gerry that he was confused about why Gerry decided to live the homosexual lifestyle. Other candidates included Dr. Joyce deJong, a forensic pathologist with children in the school district, and Benjamin Lilly, a 22-year old Byron Center High School graduate. deJong and Lilly opposed the efforts to drive Gerry out of the school. As others announced their candidacy throughout the spring, the media covered the election and accurately framed it around the Gerry Crane controversy. Rev. Richard Gregory, along with a half dozen other local ministers, called for each candidate to publicly announce their position about homosexuality. The ministers wrote an "Open Letter to the Community of Byron Center" urging voters "to vote for candidates who unashamedly espouse the moral standards that made our nation great." [63]

In its April 29, 1996, edition, *Time* magazine, ran a two-page article titled, "The Unmarrying Kind: Focusing on Local Targets, Religious Conservatives Wage a Fervent Campaign to Stomp Out Gay Rights," which addressed the Christian right's national strategy of concentrating on local policy and law.[64] It featured Gerry's struggle at Byron Center, as well as a controversy over anti-gay curricula at a New Hampshire school.[65] The article, which included a photograph of Gerry and Randy, referred to the video, book, and letter that was mailed to parents in Byron Center and described the situation regarding Kim, Gerry's student who told Gerry she had been pressured by her parents and church to withdraw from his class and that she had been told that her boyfriend would become gay if he stayed in Gerry's class.

With the release of this article, Skilling called Gerry into his office, along with the assistant principal. Skilling complained that the article was "controversial" and "sensational." Of course Gerry did not create the controversy, and the article included no sensational statements, only facts—facts about Gerry's commitment ceremony, facts about parents pulling their students out of his classes, facts about the school board's statement on homosexuals, facts about the anti-gay video and book mailing, facts about the flyer that referred to a "Sodomite music teacher," and facts about Gerry's reprimand regarding a student's request to drop his class—facts that on their own are dramatic.

Skilling said that it was a tense time. He spoke to Gerry as if they were in a Bible study group. "As a Christian," Skilling said, we are to "live the way God wants us to live." Skilling admonished Gerry not to force his values and beliefs on *us*. Without describing who he meant by "us," it appeared to be a reference to those in the Byron Center community—parents, students, administrators, teachers, ministers, and other residents who shared socially and religiously conservative Christian beliefs. In essence, Skilling was saying that Gerry was the problem. Skilling said that the students had experienced too much controversy, that their high school years should be the best time of their lives, and that the students had had too much. After asserting that the events of the past six months were of Gerry's making, Skilling concluded the meeting by telling Gerry that they should start meeting every week to "build trust" with each other. His reference to building trust appeared to be a response to comments by Gerry in the *Time* magazine article. Gerry had said that he did not feel safe at his school and spoke of an "an incredible aura of mistrust" in the school.[66]

The following week, the first week of May, Gerry was required to attend a meeting with Skilling. It was not, however, to engage in a trust-building session. Instead, Skilling interrogated Gerry about the *Time* magazine article. Skilling began the meeting by laying a copy of the article on the table, with the section about Kim highlighted in yellow.

Skilling asked Gerry, "How did the reporter get this information?"

Gerry's attorney responded, saying that Gerry had talked to a reporter.

Skilling asked Gerry exactly what information he had conveyed to the reporter.

Gerry said, "I don't recall. I really don't think it matters."

Skilling persisted.

Gerry said he believed it was from a different newspaper article.

"Did you verify the information?" Skilling asked.

"I was given information and the reporter asked me to confirm or deny it," Gerry said. "I wouldn't deny it."

⌒⌒

A few weeks later, after the principal completed his investigation regarding who had provided the information to the *Time* reporter, he gave Gerry a memo stating: "It appears you did not knowingly or directly provide the student information" contained in the article. But the memo emphasized, in bold font, that Gerry was expected to be accountable for the actions of others: "There is a concern that individuals acting in your behalf, may have disclosed confidential student communications inappropriately. This is a situation for which you must take responsibility in the future." The written directive that Gerry must "take responsibility" for what others were doing in reaction to the humiliation and harassment he was experiencing as a teacher was a blatant effort to pressure him to resign.

In fact this exact type of memo—encouraging the taking of responsibility for others—should have been written by the superintendent to *Principal Skilling* after employees under his supervision helped with the video and book mailing. As principal it was Skilling's job to set the tone. In the fall Skilling had told employees not to get involved in the controversy. Many teachers and employees followed that directive, including some who wanted to get involved on Gerry's behalf. However, Friddle, Reisterer, and Tom Hooker (the health and science teacher at the high school) were involved. Hooker had read Bible verses in his health class in the fall and had been actively involved in the campaign against Gerry. It was the mailing that had brought the most national attention, including the *Time* magazine article. Had Skilling taken early, decisive action against inappropriate behavior by school employees, the video and book mailing may have been stopped. Skilling was the one who needed to take responsibility for his role in the controversy.

10

Lyrics

There is a witch hunt in Byron Center that no one seems able to stop, and which they are determined will end with a lynching—if not in reality, then most certainly in spirit.

Gerry Crane

For some, the highlight of their high school years is participating in sports. For others, it's their school musical. The musical involves months of practice and includes learning new skills, preparing costumes, creating sets and props, being part of a tight-knit community, and working together every day after school. Gerry brought musical theater to the students.

In the spring of 1996, Gerry directed a student production of *South Pacific*. Set during World War II, the story is about two interracial couples. One romance is between a French man, who has biracial children, and a white American Navy nurse. The second storyline follows the relationship between a white American Marine officer and a Vietnamese woman. The musical was first performed in 1949, and its progressive racial themes made it controversial, especially in southern states.

Gerry had selected *South Pacific* for two reasons: its theme and its music. He loved the music. One song, "You've Got to Be Carefully Taught," examines the origin of prejudice, describing how children are taught by their family to hate and fear the despised classes of people. Gerry typically made his music selections for the school year during the summer months, as was the case with this musical.

In need of a choreographer, Gerry thought of David Watt, whom he had met when volunteering at Westminster's food pantry in the early 1990s. The two men had a number of things in common: they were both gay and had attended Calvin College; they both sought and found a more accepting church at Westminster Presbyterian Church; and they both worked as music educators.

Gerry remembered that Dave had choreographed *South Pacific* the year before at Muskegon Community College, so he called him to see if they could meet for coffee. When they got together, after catching up, Gerry told Dave that he was doing a musical at school.

"Which one?" Dave asked.

"South Pacific."

Dave smiled.

"Would you do the choreography?" Gerry asked.

Dave eagerly responded, "Sure."

When Dave told Gerry that his fee was five hundred dollars, Gerry laughed. "That's more than our entire budget. The students are amazing. You'll love working with them. And don't worry I'll be at every rehearsal."

"I'm in," Dave replied. "I'll do it for gas money."

They immediately dove into an animated discussion about the production. They also discussed the need for Dave to not disclose his sexual orientation or discuss any gay-related topics with the students.

All the students in the musical had chosen to be there; none were required by the school to participate. They were committed and wanted the performance to be successful, in part to support their besieged teacher and showcase his talents.

Gerry loved it. The rehearsals were the highlight of his day. He finally could be himself at school. Immersing himself in his work was the way he had learned to deal with the stress. Without a large budget, Gerry was the director, pianist, chorus director, orchestra director, and lead prop constructor. Dave was the choreographer, and another friend active in community theater helped with scene work. Greg Reinstein, an art teacher at the school, helped with the props.

"Gerry was very organized and energized. He was an incredible teacher. It was a blast for everyone," Dave said.

Having witnessed the way Gerry was being treated, students needed to have a measure of courage to join this production. Some received flak from their peers for participating.

Brian Jauw, one of the students in the musical, explained, "It was not unusual for two friends to have opposing views about Mr. Crane. Many of us had a silent agreement not to talk about it. We recognized that we would not be changing the other person's view."

However, not all students took this approach. While walking home after rehearsal one day, someone drove past Brian and yelled, "Fag!"

"For those of us who supported Mr. Crane, by the time practice began for the spring musical, we had learned to grow thick skin," Brian said.

At the end of each rehearsal, Gerry gave the students a short motivational talk. At times the students would break out in applause.

"You are brave to be on stage. You need to say, 'Yes, I'm in the musical' and be proud of it. Hold your head high about what you're doing. We will do our best and put it out there," Gerry said to the students.

As the performance dates drew near, he said, "On opening night, when those curtains open, you will be so proud."

Brian reflected years later: "Mr. Crane was very demanding. He had high standards and we worked really hard. Yet we had a lot of fun."

To provide the students with an audience during rehearsals, Gerry brought a stuffed toy version of Jack Skellington—the tall, thin, ghoulish character from the 1993 film *The Nightmare Before Christmas*—and placed "Skully," as he named him, in a chair directly in front of the stage.

Gerry and Dave also challenged students to be a little outrageous and work both ends of the gender spectrum. One day Dave was working with a group of girls on the song "I'm Gonna Wash That Man Right Outa My Hair." He gave each girl a towel to hold during this piece. Before he demonstrated the dance style, Dave told them, "I'm going to flame out, and you need to be even more feminine than me."

In the last week of rehearsal, during this song Gerry jumped up on stage and said to the girls, "You've got to do it like this," showing them a series of sassy, hyper-feminine moves, poses, and gestures, ending on the ground with a head snap. The girls loved it.

The musical also calls for strong, masculine performances for the songs "There Is Nothin' Like a Dame" and "Bloody Mary." Dave had the boys emphasize the characters' masculinity by using strong arm gestures, stomping their feet, and falling into a push-up position.

During one comedic scene, the character Luther Billis plays Honey Bun, a woman, wearing a blond wig, a grass skirt, and a coconut-shell bra, and dances with the Polynesian women. Gerry took pains to make sure that James Morin, the student playing Luther, was comfortable in the role. Gerry had James wear a shirt under his coconut top, unlike the character in the Broadway production and film.

On opening night, however, James shocked everyone, including his teacher, when he came out on stage shirtless except for the coconut-shell bra and gave an energetic, over-the-top performance. At one point he eyed one of the high school teachers who had expressed anti-gay beliefs and blew him a kiss. Gerry noticed this, looked down, and shook his head.

The musical was a great success. Many of Gerry's friends from Westminster Presbyterian and from AWARE attended and were thrilled to see Gerry in his element. Rev. Knieriemen from Westminster saw the show and thought, *How brilliant! How could they let him go?* Randy also attended the show; he made sure to go with their friend Marian Vanderwall because attending with a woman was a safeguard of sorts.

For days that spring, Gerry soaked in the joy and satisfaction of directing the student musical.

The musical itself represented a type of Rorschach test. Many thought Gerry used *South Pacific* to undermine parental authority and their religious beliefs about homosexuality. They rejected any analogy between racism and homophobia. They felt it was inappropriate for a high school production to include drag with a male character wearing a grass skirt and coconut-shell top. More specifically, it was inappropriate for an outed gay teacher to do so. Others, however, appreciated how the musical challenged people to think about what happens when a romantic relationship undermines the notion of socially acceptable love. The lyrics spoke to the core of the Byron Center controversy: parents were teaching their children to hate and fear.

A student writer for the school yearbook asked Gerry for his comments about the performance. He gave the response he was known for and that his students had come to love: "It was fab-u-lous!"

Next, it was time for the choir's spring concert. As part of the program, the students sang "Colors of the Wind" from the Disney movie *Pocahontas*. In this song, Pocahontas, a Native American, sings about her experience with white people. She explains that white people do not respect Native Americans or nature, and urges them to walk in the shoes of people who are different from them, to witness the lives of animals, and to fully experience nature. The lyrics also crystalize this point—prejudice causes emotional and physical pain. Not surprisingly, many framed Gerry's selection of this well-loved Disney song as another example of insubordination.

Since October 1995, the voices of those who believed that homosexuality was a sin had filled the newspapers. These letters often started with the phrases "as a Christian" or "I'm a Christian." A small group of local ministers were frustrated. The letters left people with the impression that *all* Christians condemned homosexuality, while these ministers believed that homosexuality was not a sin. Their Christian belief was that gay people were children of God, created in God's image.

Spurred by what they saw as the co-opting of Christianity to condemn Gerry, it was time, they concluded, to do more. They wanted to build awareness and educate people about the theological basis for their belief. At the same time, Rev. Knieriemen expressed her concern that Rev. Evertsberg was taking all the public heat for his support of same-sex unions.

One afternoon in late winter, these ministers gathered for lunch on the sun porch at Gibson's restaurant to discuss ways to gather and formalize a network of like-minded ministers.

The restaurant was located in an Italianate-style mansion that had a religious history—it once housed Benedictine friars and, at a later time, Franciscan priests.

Sitting around the table were seven ministers: Rev. Evertsberg, Rev. Knieriemen, Rev. Douglas Van Doren of Plymouth United Church of Christ, Rev. Ronald Skidmore of South Congregational United Church of Christ, Rev. Kenneth Gottman of United Church of Christ, Rev. Brian Byrne of East Congregational United Church of Christ, and Rev. Sue Sinnamon of Fountain Street Church. Rev. Van Doren had a history of strong social justice work. His was a lived faith, ministering to people in his congregation and advocating for racial equity, LGBTQ+ rights, immigrant rights, peace, and reproductive freedom.

It was not surprising that four of the ministers at the meeting were from the United Church of Christ (UCC). The UCC's historical roots extend to abolition, Women's Suffrage, civil rights, reproductive justice, and the right to be a conscientious objector. The UCC was also a forerunner in gay rights, ordaining its first openly gay minister in 1972. Three years later the UCC passed a resolution condemning discrimination based on "affectional or sexual preference." One minister in the group was from Fountain Street Church, a religiously liberal non-denominational church founded in 1869, with a rich history of engaging in progressive thought and social justice action.[67]

Their conversation flowed effortlessly. They shared a frustration that Christianity was being used to condemn Gerry. They were also pained to read letters from people who supported Gerry and condemned Christianity based on one "Christian" view.

"The issue was that people were only hearing one voice of Christianity. The conservative one dominated the coverage," Rev. Knieriemen explained.

The group knew there was a cadre of pastors who shared their belief about homosexuality and that some would be willing to speak publicly to this end. As they wrapped up, they agreed to continue their discussion at monthly lunch meetings. Each minister made a commitment to invite more ministers.

This group, which began as "Concerned Pastors," later changed its name to Concerned Clergy of West Michigan. The ministers held their first official meeting at Westminster. They invited other ministers and succeeded in expanding their numbers. The group developed four objectives:

1. offering support for and sharing the ways their congregations are involved with issues of homosexuality and the church to discover ways the church could become more faithful to calls to inclusivity;
2. sharing their denominations' study documents on becoming open, welcoming, and affirming for gay people;[68]
3. sharing information on "conservative" communities where "liberal" pastors have organized; and
4. drafting a statement to express their beliefs and actions, to make public at the right time.

This group continued to reach out to others they thought would share their objectives. One of their main priorities was to write a "pastoral letter" from the group to be publicized to all of west Michigan.

These ministers represented a variety of denominations and, as would be expected, brought their unique denominational perspectives to the content and wording of the letter. The group engaged in many careful discussions about the language. In late May, Rev. Bill Evertsberg and Rev. Linda Knieriemen sent a note to everyone in the group. It began, "Alleluia, it's done!" The final version of the pastoral letter was attached.

A Pastoral Letter from Concerned Clergy
in West Michigan

We are a group of Christian pastors and church leaders of several denominations. We are concerned about what has often been represented as the only Christian response toward gay and lesbian people.

The intolerance and exclusivity of this response grieve us because we see it as a misinterpretation of the gospel's call for the church to be the "body of Christ." This misinterpretation daily wounds people both within and outside the body.

Therefore, we feel the need to voice our convictions.

We find through careful biblical study that the New Testament portrays Jesus as one who continually challenged the religious community of his day to expand the boundaries of whom they found acceptable in the Realm of God. He brought into the religious community those who had previously been labeled "impure," "unworthy," or "unclean."

We also find through careful biblical study that the few references in Scripture to same-sex sexual relationships do not have application to committed, loving same-sex relationships as they are known today. Jesus himself is silent on the issue. His call to follow his demonstrated ethic of inclusive love, however, is clear. This must be the ethic that governs Christian action. This is gospel. This is Good News.

Therefore, to be faithful to this good news:

> We call the Church to repent and hear the voices of people long silenced or excluded from full and open participation. We believe it is to the peril of the Church that it neglects the

humanity and gifts of people strictly on the basis of sexual orientation.

We call the Church to humility and to the realization that in the past it has often judged and excluded people and their viewpoints in ways we now understand to have been misguided and rooted in fear and prejudice.

We call the Church to nurture a faith that is not so insecure as to be threatened by human differences in expressing committed love. We call the churches to encourage all people, regardless of sexual orientation, to engage in sexual activity only in committed, loving relationships. We believe that to accept same-sex covenantal relationships does not threaten the validity of other-sex covenantal relationships. We believe that in order to maintain committed relationships all of us continually need to seek God's spirit and to have the support of a faith community.

We are convinced that this is a faithful, Biblically-based perspective that has compelling integrity and is shared by large numbers of thoughtful, committed Christians in many denominations.

We invite all who share this perspective to participate with us in forming strong and diverse congregations which are increasingly open and inclusive and where the healing and loving Spirit of God in Christ is honored and trusted beyond all fear and prejudice. Speaking to our churches, not necessarily for our churches, we are ...

The pastoral letter was signed by thirty-two local ministers from a variety of denominations—Presbyterian Church (USA), United Church of Christ, Episcopal Church, Universal Fellowship of Metropolitan Community Churches, United Methodist

Church—as well as clergy from Fountain Street Church and from Christ Community Church of Spring Lake, affiliated at that time with the Reformed Church in America (RCA).[69]

It was risky for many of the ministers to sign the statement. Thus, the last line—"Speaking to our churches, not necessarily for our churches"—was included. Some ministers needed to obtain permission from their church board before signing the statement. Other ministers privately supported Concerned Clergy but did not sign the statement, as they would lose their ministerial employment or risk losing their ministerial status within their denomination. This was particularly the case for those in the Reformed Church of America (RCA) and Christian Reformed Church in North America (CRC). Some ministers expressed concern that signing the statement might jeopardize funding for an inner-city church agency which served the needs of marginalized communities—funds which came from people and organizations with anti-gay beliefs.

Despite this climate, after the publication of the pastoral statement, other ministers expressed an interest in signing on. Eventually, the signatories totaled fifty-seven ministers representing more than seven denominations and over seventeen local churches.

Albert M. Lewis, serving at the time as rabbi of Temple Emanuel, a Reform Jewish community, shared the spirit of the statement. He did not sign the statement because it was written to express the beliefs of Christian clergy. His voice, however, was valued and furthered the objective of educating people about diverse religious beliefs relating to homosexuality.

Concerned Clergy reached out to Charles Honey, editor of the religion section of *The Grand Rapids Press*. At the time, the religion section was recognized as one of the best in the country. On June 2, a week before the Byron Center school board election, the *Press* published Concerned Clergy's pastoral letter, and

Honey wrote an article about it. Rev. Linda Stoner, minister at Reconciliation Metropolitan Community Church, described the letter as an affirmation for those in the gay community who were "battered and bruised by their traditional religion."[70] Those who wanted Gerry fired because of their religious beliefs, however, criticized Concerned Clergy's statement as being contrary to their interpretation of the Bible.

Gerry told Honey that he welcomed the pastoral letter, while pointing out that having a gay-affirming pastor did not necessarily mean all parishioners shared that view. Gerry explained the dilemma of being a gay person attending a "welcoming" church: "Are they going to welcome you in and hope you change? Or welcome you in and treat you like the body of Christ, like they would anybody else who walked in the door?"[71]

On June 3, Gerry had another meeting with the principal. Gerry's union representative was also present. The principal said that some students had complained about him and his musical selections and that his discussion about the music focused on tolerance and diversity. Gerry asked for a written copy of these complaints, and the principal said he would put them in writing.

After school the next day, Gerry and his attorney met with the principal. When they sat down, Gerry noticed that the principal had a list of questions in front of him. Gerry asked for a copy of these questions. Skilling denied this request, explaining that the questions were based on student complaints. Then he asked Gerry whether he had spoken to students about homosexuality, tolerance, or acceptance of his lifestyle in the classroom, in a small group, or individually, since "the November 22 directive," referring to the memo he had written to Gerry telling him that he could neither counsel students about their sexuality nor talk to them about his sexuality.

Gerry told the principal that he regularly talks to students about diversity and tolerance of all people. The principal asked Gerry if he ever taught students to accept his lifestyle or taught tolerance for homosexuality.

"I advocate a respect for diversity of any kind," Gerry said. "I have not, to the best of my knowledge, discussed my life with anyone."

Skilling asked Gerry whether diversity and tolerance was a part of the music curriculum.

"Diversity and tolerance are teachable values that supersede any curriculum content," Gerry said. "We teach that lying, stealing, racism, and sexism are wrong."

Skilling asked Gerry if he comments favorably or unfavorably on news articles.

"Students constantly ask for my perspective. It's not unusual for students to bring up news reports and for students who didn't hear about it to ask questions. I tell them to read and watch for themselves."

Skilling moved to another topic, asking Gerry if he ever made comments about the body of a male student, who was dating one of his female students. Apparently, someone made a complaint about this.

Gerry told Skilling that students often show him their prom photographs and senior pictures. "I comment in a positive way. Never with sexual comments," Gerry stated.

The principal asked Gerry if he remembered an incident when a student in his class called another student a "faggot."

"Why is this a complaint?" asked Gerry.

Skilling asserted that he was told to ask this question, that the board told him he had to monitor the situation, and that he only followed up when he received complaints.

"There have been a few instances where the term 'faggot' or 'gay' was used in a derogatory sense. I have always, and will always, stop that abuse and correct it."

"Do you recall saying, 'There's nothing wrong with being gay'?" Skilling asked.

"As a response to the derogatory comment 'faggot,' I stated that it's okay to be gay—just as I would say that to call someone the n-word is intolerable and it's okay to be black."

By early June, the school year ended, but for Gerry the repercussions continued.

Byron Center's school board election was held on June 10. Twenty-five percent of the school district's 11,727 registered voters cast their ballots—a marked increase from the usual turnout for a school board election. The most outspoken anti-gay candidates were Marvin Schierbeek and Dean Sullivan, and the voters elected both by a large margin (voters could vote for up to two candidates). The election results were:

Marvin Schierbeek...1,734

Dean Sullivan 1,422

David Flietstra (incumbent) 687

Joyce L. deJong 565

Scott Vinkemulder..563

Mike Marshall 531

Benjamin J. Lilly..199

In response to his and Schierbeek's win, Sullivan said, "We're happy that the Lord has put us in a position to be on the school board, and we'll leave it at that. God gets all the glory."

The election results were a blow to Gerry and his supporters. They had flirted with the possibility that in the privacy of the voting booth, a silent majority would voice their opposition to the board's pronouncement that a gay teacher is an inappropriate role model.

On June 24, the principal wrote a three-page memo to Gerry concluding that although there were some common facts in each of the complaints he had received about Gerry, "the details regarding most of them are in conflict, and, therefore, inconclusive as to whether any misconduct has occurred." However, the principal also wrote that based on their investigation, Gerry needed instruction on how to conduct himself in the classroom. He wrote:

> You are to teach only Board-approved curriculum. During our meeting on June 4, 1996, when questioned about whether you had been discussing your background with students, you replied, "I have always taught my students that respect for diversity is a sign of maturity and that tolerance is for all people." "I advocate a diversity of any kind." "Tolerance and diversity are teachable values that supersede any curriculum content."

> The investigation disclosed that many of your music selections and discussions of those selections with students focused on the issue of tolerance and acceptance of all people. Given your very public statements advocating acceptance and tolerance of homosexuals, your admitted advocating in the classroom of diversity of any kind and tolerance for all people, may well be interpreted as teaching tolerance and acceptance for the

homosexual lifestyle. This is counter to the Board's position, my directives, and your role as a professional teacher in this District.

In the future, please confine your teaching to the stated curriculum and curriculum objectives. If you find a need to supplement or expand the curriculum, the materials and objectives should receive prior approval.

On the same day, the principal suspended Gerry for three days without pay. The suspension memo stated that he would not serve the suspension until November 18, 19, and 20, and if there were no further problems with Gerry's performance between now and then, Skilling would suspend the suspension. If there were future violations, Gerry would serve the suspension, and Skilling would recommend his dismissal.

The stated reason for the three-day suspension was for repeatedly disregarding the principal's directive to not discuss or promote homosexuality in school. The principal wrote in a separate memo: "I want to emphasize that it was appropriate for you to advise the student that it was unacceptable to call another student a 'faggot.' Students should be held accountable and appropriately disciplined if they call any student a derogatory name. However, proceeding to inform the class 'There is nothing wrong with being gay,' interjected your personal view and opinion, which you have been directed to keep out of the school environment.... Any further violations will result in my recommendation for your dismissal."

Skilling made his position clear. Gerry, the gay teacher, failed to follow the school board's approved curriculum when he selected and discussed music which "focused on the issue of tolerance and acceptance of all people." Teaching tolerance violated Byron Center's approved curriculum.

11

Collective Musical Hug

Since the exposure, I have been the object of public debate. I have been called "immoral," accused of "espousing homosexuality," and of "encouraging and condoning" immoral conduct on the part of students. The school board, in its statement to the public, has diminished all that I am—a man, a teacher, a son and brother, a friend—degraded all that I have offered my students previously and all that I have left to offer. It has reduced all the values, skills, and abilities that make up a person to a single modifier that seems to tell them all they need to know: homosexual.

Gerry Crane

At the December 1995 meeting, when the board publicly stated that Gerry was not a proper role model for students, it cut to his core. It was an assault on his character and it degraded his value as a human being. At that time, however, he could not have known what his life would look like during the balance of the school year. Before his commitment ceremony, Gerry had never been disciplined. Between the end of October 1995 and the spring of 1996, thirteen complaints were made about Gerry. With every complaint, Gerry had to submit to interrogation by an antagonistic principal, followed by a series of meetings, knowing that the school board and administrators wanted each complaint to be the one that broke him. He was defending himself, attempting to keep his job, whack-a-mole style. The cumulative effect of these attacks was painful and eventually unbearable.

Blame cannot simply be placed on the anti-gay forces in the community. The district's intent was unmistakable. An organized, determined group of administrators and staff, along with the school board, were laser-focused on a common mission: to run him out of their school. They wanted him to resign, but he had refused. They wore him down and tried to create what they believed to be a basis to terminate his employment. The unrelenting process would either break his determination to weather the storm or they would eventually find a way to get rid of him.

The district demonstrated this intent not only with their actions but also their inaction. In the face of ongoing public attack and controversy, the district did not praise Gerry—either publicly or within the school community—for his steadfast devotion to his teaching, along with his commitment to the students' successful concerts and school musical. They never acknowledged, publicly or privately, that Gerry was not the person who had brought his private life into the classroom. They never developed a plan to support Gerry as a highly acclaimed and positively reviewed teacher, amidst the public attacks against him.

They did not reach out or take actions to support students who identified as gay or who might have been be in the process of coming to terms with their own sexuality. They did not ask students who supported Gerry to write letters to the media about their positive experience with their teacher. They did not bring speakers into the school or require students to hear presentations about the Constitutional separation of religion and public education.

There was a theory in the community that those who wanted Gerry fired were a small but vocal group, and that the problem was that the silent majority was afraid to publicly speak up. Gerry shared this belief. Yet the June 10 school board election said otherwise. Voters overwhelmingly supported the two candidates who had vocalized the position that religion—specifically, conservative Christian doctrine—should be considered when making decisions about school policy and, in particular, policies involving gay teachers. Gerry was stunned and hurt by the election results. Given the opportunity to voice their views in the privacy of the voting booth, the people of Byron Center had made it clear that they did not want this gay teacher in their district.

Gerry knew the election would empower school officials. And he was correct. They considered firing him immediately, but they were concerned that Gerry would file a lawsuit. They decided that they needed to build their case against him, while continuing to hope that he would resign. A few weeks after the board election, Gerry was given the three-day suspension for "disregarding the principal's directive to not discuss or promote homosexuality in the classroom."

The district and others opposing Gerry had actually begun exploring potential legal arguments for terminating his employment only weeks after his commitment ceremony in October 1995. One argument floated was based on Gerry's private sex life. That Gerry admitted he had participated in a commitment ceremony with another man—the argument went—was evidence that he was engaging in sex with another man in violation of Michigan's sodomy law. The Michigan law "Crime Against Nature or Sodomy" states that any person "who shall commit the abominable and detestable crime against nature either with mankind or with any animal" is guilty of a felony.[72] As a person engaging in *criminal behavior*, Gerry should be terminated. The argument was that homosexuality was not only a sin under their religious beliefs, but it was also a felony under state law.

At least one person in the community suggested that this law could be the basis to fire Gerry unless he agreed to "testify" to the school board that he was in a celibate relationship. This line of thinking was hypocritical. Someone who thought that a gay teacher was an inappropriate role model for students thought that it was moral to attempt to coerce someone to speak to the school board about his sex life. Another suggested legal argument was based on the inaccurate claim that Gerry was the person who brought the topic of his commitment ceremony—his private life—into the school and into the classroom. By doing so, he had created a controversy and a disruption, which caused students to be pulled out of his classes and led to bitterness and fear among students, teachers, parents, and the community; it also wasted the time of school administrators and destroyed school spirit and unity. And Gerry was responsible for causing elementary students to lose their innocence because parents had to talk to their children about homosexuality.

However, the administration knew as early as August 1995 that Gerry's personal life had been brought into the school not by Gerry but by a number of parents. By October they knew it was a student who had snuck into Gerry's private commitment ceremony to take a program. And they knew that it was another student (whose parents wanted Gerry fired) who had brought up the topic in class by asking Gerry about the ring on his finger and asking what he had done that weekend. Gerry did not engage in a discussion about his personal life or about homosexuality with his class; instead, after his life became the talk of the school, he said to his students, "Should it matter? If not, then I have a job to do and you have a job to do. Let's get to it."[73]

In fact, Gerry and Randy, as a couple, had taken affirmative steps to keep their relationship out of Gerry's workplace. They had included the words "confidentiality is appreciated" on the invitation to their commitment ceremony. During the school board meeting held in the gym in December 1995, which was attended by over seven hundred people, Gerry chose not to sit with Randy in the bleachers; instead, in the presence of his students, he had to watch and listen to the board, administrators, colleagues, parents, students, and ministers give their opinions about him. Having Randy sitting next to him would have been comforting and supportive. However, Gerry and Randy chose not to sit together, stand together, hug, or exchange words of encouragement. They even drove to the board meeting in separate cars and did not walk into the school together. Randy had to watch the man he loved be publicly demeaned, ridiculed, and harassed because of *their* commitment ceremony. While Randy would have been justified in doing so, he did not speak at the meeting about the controversy. They had taken every step possible to keep their personal relationship out of the school.

Gerry's private relationship had not affected his performance as a teacher. He had continued to excel in spite of the chaos around him. While Michigan law did not prohibit employment discrimination based on a person's sexual orientation, there were no Michigan cases supporting the firing of a teacher for merely being gay. This does not mean teachers were never fired for merely being gay; it means that gay teachers did not challenge a firing because to do so would "out" them to family, friends, and neighbors and would most likely close doors to future employment as a teacher.

If Gerry were fired, the legal question would be decided based on both the teacher tenure law and the union contract. Because Gerry had tenure, the district would have to prove that it had "just cause" to terminate his employment. But the district held all the political and financial power. They had a fervent collection of board members, administrators, staff, and parents who were committed to fighting until Gerry was gone. They had even shown their willingness to pressure certain students to act as their foot soldiers.

While the district was pondering ways to force Gerry to leave, he was considering his options. He assumed that no school district in the area would hire him, the demonized "gay music teacher." Even if a district had an opening and valued Gerry's work, he assumed they would not want to bring controversy—along with the wrath of the religious right and all the media coverage—to their school. Plus, local job openings for high school music teachers were quite limited, even in the best years.

The idea of resigning was incompatible with the essence of his being. However, he had to face reality. There were no Michigan or federal statutes or cases protecting employees from discrimination based on sexual orientation. One option was for Gerry to file a lawsuit against the district claiming he was being discriminated against based on his sexual orientation, in violation of his rights to due process and equal protection. There were legal arguments to support this type of claim, but given the state of the law, coupled with the number of conservative judges in the state and federal courts, the odds would have been against him. Another legal option was to file a lawsuit based on constructive discharge, which applies if an employee resigns because an employer made working conditions so intolerable that a reasonable person would feel that they were compelled to resign. This reasonably described the district's actions during the previous year. But this argument would need to be based on a court's finding that the district violated Gerry's rights to due process or equal protection.

Gerry had to also consider how long that legal process would take. Given that the school board, along with many other supporting organizations, would fund and pursue appeals, the process could take as much as three to seven years. Gerry also needed to consider the cultural climate of the community: his being gay would be the center of his lawsuit, and potential jurors and judges—from the mostly conservative religious community—would clearly lean in favor of the school district.

Finally, there were personal and professional considerations. A lawsuit of this nature is grueling—Gerry's life would continue to be consumed by the district. He would need to participate in endless meetings, depositions, court hearings, settlement conferences, and ultimately a trial. He would need to read and respond to school documents, transcripts, and court documents; he would be subjected to cross-examination and would need to defend himself against false accusations. Some of his colleagues, his former and current students, and their parents would likely sign affidavits and testify against him. His attorney would need to ask other colleagues and students to testify about facts necessary to counter false allegations. The process would be covered by the media. And, such a lawsuit would likely close doors to other teaching opportunities. Perhaps after a couple of years, a district might hire him, but there was no guarantee. The situation was overwhelming.

⁓

With the end of the school year in June, however, the decision could wait. The strain of the prior seven months had taken a toll on Gerry and Randy's relationship. At times Gerry had tried to protect Randy from the turbulence and stress of his daily life. In doing so, however, to some extent he was pushing Randy away. He wasn't always good at accepting Randy's support. More than anything, however, it was Gerry's career, and he had to make decisions on a regular basis.

In June, Gerry and Randy embarked on a long-anticipated, two-week trip to the Massachusetts coast. It was a relief to leave Michigan and simply enjoy their relationship. As they drove east, the protective armor Gerry had been wearing for months started to melt away. After twelve hours on the road, they were close to Boston. While Randy was driving, Gerry broke down in tears, "I just realized this is the first day since this started last fall that I don't have a headache."

They spent most of their time on the coast. The rhythmic sound of the waves and the feel of the gentle sea breeze and sunshine was cleansing and freeing. Gerry resurrected his capacity to relax. He was able to celebrate what was good in his life—his relationship with Randy and others close to him.

Yet Byron Center hovered over their get-away. Gerry needed to make a decision about his employment. Should he return to school in the fall? Resign? Pursue legal action? This vacation was the first time since their commitment ceremony that Gerry was able to reflect on what had happened to him while not having to steel himself to focus on daily school matters. They talked about Gerry's struggle, about the effect it had on Gerry and on their relationship. During their vacation they talked to Gerry's attorneys—Bill Young with the MEA, David Buckel and Patricia Logue at Lambda Legal, and with the people at the Human Rights Campaign—discussing strategies and options.

In addition to the emotional stress, Gerry had unwillingly become the poster boy for gay-related employment discrimination, and together Gerry and Randy had become the poster couple. Their life had become an important story for gay rights organizations to discuss and promote. While Gerry valued the activism of those who fought for equality, it was antithetical to his own personality. However, once he was propelled into the gay rights arena, he understood the value of his experience for the movement. His experience could become a test case for the employment rights of gay people. He wanted to do what he could for the movement. He also felt a pressure to do so. But these attorneys did not sugarcoat the litigation process. At a minimum it would require him to return to school in the fall, and the process would take years. He would be propelled further into the national limelight. All of this would distract him from his life's work—to teach high school music. And there were no guarantees he would win the fight.

After more reflection and discussion with Randy, Gerry could not ignore the fact that the past school year had ravaged his life. By the end of their vacation, a decision had crystalized for Gerry. He realized that what was at stake was his humanity—his value as a kind, compassionate, loving human being and a skilled and dedicated teacher.

When they returned to Michigan, Gerry told his attorney he had decided to resign.

Bill Young contacted the school's attorney, and a settlement was negotiated. As is often the case, Gerry, the employee, did not have equal bargaining power with his employer. In most cases a large corporation, or in this case a governmental entity, holds most of the bargaining power in a discrimination case. Decisions are made by a small number of people at the top and, in the case of governmental units, with the approval of a board and input from their attorney. These people have job security, the strength and confidence that comes with being the small group that holds the power, and the ability to continue to engage in the actions, such as discrimination or retaliation, that lead to the need for a settlement or lawsuit. The employee has little power, and, in fact, the employee risks their current and future income, their reputation, and their confidence, along with risking the loss of engaging in work that they are trained to do, work that may even give them meaning in life and, as in Gerry's case, work that they relish. The employee also carries the emotional and physical pain that results from discrimination, harassment, and retaliation.

Gerry's only leverage was that they wanted him to resign. But once Gerry's attorney contacted the district in July to inform them that Gerry wanted to resign, they had him over a barrel. If he tried to negotiate a better settlement package and they held firm, Gerry would have to continue teaching in the fall and be subjected to the disciplinary action imposed in late June and to ongoing harassment and attacks. The school would not have stopped until they pushed him out or fired him.

The final agreement between Gerry and the district required the district to pay Gerry one year's salary, approximately $43,700, less taxes and related deductions, prorated over the next school year, and to maintain his health care coverage over this time. The grievances that Gerry had filed in February and June—challenging the discipline about how he had handled a student's drop slip and his three-day suspension for how he had responded to a student who had called another student a "faggot"—would be decided by arbitration. If the arbitrator concluded that the disciplinary actions were not legitimate, the district would be required to remove the disciplinary documents from Gerry's file. It was important for Gerry to challenge these disciplinary actions in order to clear his personnel record for future employment. The school was also required to write a mutually-agreed-on reference letter for Gerry.

For his part, Gerry agreed to resign and to waive his right to sue the district for discrimination, breach of contract, defamation, or a denial of his constitutional rights. Gerry also had to make "good-faith efforts" in the coming year to obtain employment, and any income he earned would offset and reduce the amount of district's payments. While this "offset" provision is often used in employment cases, it favors employers and reflects the superior bargaining power of employers and insurance companies.

Gerry had to agree that he would not apply for employment within the school district in the future and to acknowledge that the district had no obligation to consider him for reemployment.

Gerry and the board mutually agreed to refrain from publicly disparaging each other.

On July 26, Gerry drove to the school and turned in his signed resignation agreement—one year after he had called a musician to ask her to perform at his commitment ceremony. As Gerry drove away from the school, he passed Jim Jauw's house and saw that Jim was outside. Jim and his wife, Kathy, had two kids in band and they had consistently supported Gerry throughout the previous year. Gerry pulled over and told Jim that he had just turned in his resignation. They talked for a few minutes.

Before leaving, Gerry said, "Please support the kids and program in any way you can."

The board was required to formally approve the settlement agreement at their next meeting in August. Byron Center parent and former school board candidate, Dr. Joyce L. deJong, wrote to the school board, "I hereby make a formal appeal to the board members to publicly apologize to Mr. Crane for the treatment he has suffered at your hands. I challenge you to apologize to him. I challenge you to stand up to the legal recommendations of your legal counsel and apologize." There was no apology.

Instead, during the meeting a school representative commented that the settlement was fair for both Gerry and the district, adding that it was similar to what they would pay a teacher who was terminated for misconduct. He then clarified that Gerry was not being accused of misconduct. The comment sounded like spin to appease those who thought Gerry should have been fired without pay, while implying that Gerry's settlement amount was standard.

In fact, the settlement was not fair for Gerry. He should have been paid significantly more than a teacher accused of misconduct. A just resolution would have been for the board to withdraw their December 1995 statement that homosexuals are not a proper role model for teachers, publicly apologize to Gerry, withdraw their discipline from his personnel file, and pay him more money. The amount should have included at least two years of salary to give him a more reasonable amount of time to try to obtain another job as a music teacher, and a large sum as compensation for the discrimination and retaliation.

At the same meeting, Principal Skilling praised Gerry for the outstanding organizational structure he had put in place which would benefit the band students at camp the following week.

And so it went—Gerry's year of hell at the hands of Skilling and others was thus sandwiched between Skilling's glowing performance evaluation of Gerry in July 1995 and Skilling's final statement in August 1996 praising Gerry's talents as a teacher.

School officials, some of Gerry's colleagues, and offended parents and ministers had accomplished their goal. They didn't hate him—some of them said—they loved him. They had wanted him out of their school, and the outed gay teacher finally left. They were done condemning Gerry Crane.

At least for now.

Gerry's life had been filled with music since his early childhood. Performing, studying, teaching, and directing music in choirs, bands, and orchestras fueled Gerry's zest for life. Even during the difficulties of the preceding school year, Gerry's commitment to and love of teaching had replenished his soul. It had helped him to continue to move forward. In his darkest days, the deep satisfaction he felt from seeing his students' progress was his lifeline. Teaching music was Gerry's oxygen.

He had not had time during the school year to distill the traumatic events happening to him. To be able to focus on his work, he had masked his frustration, anger, and pain. He now needed to see a therapist. He started a grueling, yet necessary, process of delving into his disbelief, sadness, betrayal, anger, and rage.

That summer as Gerry started to focus on reclaiming his life and making plans for the future, he still had to deal with Byron Center. Gerry remained a news item throughout June, July, and August. The media had covered the school board elections and had connected the results to Gerry; they reported the school's decision in June to give him a three-day suspension; and they covered his resignation. After every article, more people wrote letters to the local paper, expressing their opinions about Gerry the teacher and Gerry the homosexual.

⌒⌒

Tammy Lee, Gerry's student who had watched the propaganda video sent to her home and had discovered a wider LGBTQ+ culture, was becoming more comfortable with being open about her sexuality. She was upset when she heard that Gerry had resigned. She understood why he had made the decision, but she was angry about the way he had been treated by the school.

One afternoon in late summer, Tammy went with a friend to a gay bar in downtown Grand Rapids, the Carousel. As the two sat talking and smoking, someone suddenly reached from behind Tammy, grabbed the cigarette from between her fingers, and drove it into the ash tray on her table. She turned around. It was Gerry.

"You'll never do that again," Gerry said, with his trademark raised eyebrow.

Gerry was at the bar for an interview with a newspaper reporter. Gerry and Tammy talked for a few minutes and then he went to sit with the reporter.

Always the teacher, Tammy thought.

Another day Tammy and a friend showed up unannounced at Gerry's house after they found out where he lived. Gerry answered the door, holding an apple and a paring knife. He had been peeling the skin in a continuous circular manner. He greeted Tammy and her friend with an expression of surprise and delight. Gerry welcomed them in and introduced them to Randy. He invited Tammy to attend his church, to experience a church that was not judgmental toward LGBTQ+ folks. Tammy and her older brother eventually went with Gerry and Randy several times to Westminster.

～

With fall came the start of a new school year, filled with back-to-school rituals, students returning energized by the summer months, and the excitement of marching band. It was the time of year Gerry had previously relished. This fall, however, Gerry sat on the sidelines facing his pain.

When Gerry resigned, he knew he would not find work as a music teacher that year. Someone in the Forest Hills school district, also located in Kent County, made overtures to Gerry that they would like to hire him but that they would need to wait for publicity to wane before considering such a hire. This gave him a small measure of hope, but Forest Hills was a wealthy, popular district with limited teacher turnover. Would there actually be an opening? How many years would it take? And while Gerry could reasonably expect more support from the Forest Hills district, there would still be a strong, vocal opposition.

Gerry needed to explore other options. He began taking classes in pursuit of a master's in social work at Western Michigan University, located fifty miles south of Grand Rapids in Kalamazoo. One of Gerry's strengths was connecting with students and adults in a meaningful way. But this did not solve the core problem: school districts who did not want to hire Gerry to teach music would also not want to hire him to counsel their students. His ability to find employment would be limited to a district willing to take on the blowback and media attention that would follow.

Prior to resigning from Byron Center, Gerry had taught individual music lessons. He took on additional students after he had resigned and also directed a local lesbian and gay chorus. Gerry also volunteered at his church's food pantry, often working there with Bruce Wilcox, a friend who had recently left his full-time work because of a health problem. Gerry and Bruce shared similar experiences as gay, Christian men navigating life in west Michigan, while adjusting to loss of employment for reasons beyond their control. Bruce was a sounding board for Gerry. They buoyed each other's spirits and often worked out together at the YMCA.

∼

As fall approached, Gerry had to prepare for the arbitration hearing, which was scheduled for September and later adjourned to November 29, to challenge the disciplinary actions taken against him. He needed to arbitrate to clear his personnel file for future employment and to fight for at least a small measure of justice.

Four months had passed since Gerry resigned—he had started to get some distance from the events of the prior school year. The arbitration, however, meant that he had to relive in detail the events that caused him to resign, including the meetings with Skilling questioning him about the latest accusations—meetings that were difficult to endure the first time. In addition, the school included in their exhibits disparaging, false, and hurtful gossip about Gerry—gossip that did not relate to Gerry's work or his students.

The school's attorney argued that the discipline was not about his homosexuality but rather about Gerry not following directions and restrictions. Of course, these special directions were given and the restrictions were put in place for the sole reason that Gerry was gay. As Gerry repeatedly heard his name associated with "the controversy," he wrote on a piece of paper: "Why am I responsible for the controversy?"

After the hearing, the arbitrator told the attorneys to submit their written arguments to him by January 10, 1997, and he would issue his decision within thirty-five days after that. Gerry would have to wait another two to three months to learn the final status of his grievances.

⌒

Martin, a student of Gerry's, was devastated by the way the school and community continued to treat his teacher. He proudly and publicly supported his teacher. Gerry had been helpful and a good listener when Martin needed to talk. Martin's girlfriend's parents had said that Gerry was an inappropriate role model for students, but Martin knew better. In September 1996, Martin, at age eighteen, died by suicide. Gerry was heartbroken. He racked his brain, wondering if he could have done something to save Martin. He went to Martin's funeral and grieved with his family and friends.

⌒

Gerry's story continued to draw people to Westminster Presbyterian Church. People came to experience a loving faith community and to support the church that was supporting Gerry and Randy. Joyce Recker was one of those people. Even though she was agnostic, she started attending Westminster at this time. During an Advent Sunday service, the congregation sang the Christmas carol *In the Bleak Midwinter*:

> In the bleak midwinter, frosty wind made moan,
> Earth stood hard as iron, water like a stone;
> Snow had fallen, snow on snow, snow on snow.
> In the bleak midwinter, long ago.[74]

Joyce stood in the pew behind Gerry, Randy, and Marian Vanderwall. It caught her attention that they were singing the hymn with joy and hope. Joyce thought, *This is such a profound metaphor. Through the bleakest time of Gerry's life, here they were, still standing, singing, and clinging to hope.*

On December 13, Gerry directed the West Michigan Gay Community Chorus in a concert, "Songs for the Holidays." The concert was held at Trinity United Methodist Church. Two of the church's ministers—Rev. Gerald Pohly and Rev. Gerald Toshalis—were a part of Concerned Clergy and had signed the group's June 1996 pastoral letter. Trinity was a "reconciling church," the term used by Methodists for a church that affirms people of all sexual orientations and gender identities.

As people walked in and took their seats in the pews for the concert, there was an air of anticipation. Beyond the usual greetings and hugs among friends, there was a broader kinship as people exchanged smiles and head nods with others who looked familiar. The experience felt personal. The reason for this familiarity slowly crystalized—the audience for the concert included some of the same people who had supported Gerry at the school board meetings and the school musical. Even the same reporters were present. But what was missing was the destructive energy. That evening everyone present valued Gerry as a loving gay man, a talented musician, and trusted friend. They had an emotional connection to him and an investment in the concert. This inspired a sense of hope.

The women and men of the chorus walked into the sanctuary and took their places on the tiered stage. Gerry, dressed in his black tuxedo, walked to the podium and faced the choir. He raised his arms with baton in hand, paused to nod at the pianist, and then directed the choir through an energized rendition of "It's the Most Wonderful Time of the Year." When they finished, they received thunderous applause. Mark Dyer, the president of the chorus, stepped forward, made welcoming remarks, and the concert began.

The members of the chorus, like his high school choir students in December 1995, had Gerry's welfare in mind during their rehearsals and concerts.

Theresa McClellan, a friend of Gerry's, a member of the chorus, and a reporter for *The Grand Rapids Press*, said, "We needed to be able to do our best. We gave him a collective musical hug."

After the concert, there was a reception at the church. The mood was festive. Those who had come to see Gerry waited their turn to talk with him. Gerry appreciated the support. He was most energized when he saw students, and the students were thrilled to see him. A small group of students made plans with Gerry and Randy to attend a music event together in January.

The concert was a night of joy and hope. Gerry the musician was back on stage.

It was also a night veiled in sadness, a reminder of all that had been lost.

12

Broken Heart

*Byron Center citizens condemn me for the choices they believe I
have made, yet they reduce me to only two choices that matter:
Go in the fire—protesting my innocence like a witch at Salem. Or
go quietly, silently—a martyr to injustice and ignorance.*

Gerry Crane

It was the Christmas season, and Gerry and Randy enjoyed their
Christmas traditions—they hosted the AWARE Christmas party,
they found comfort in their church services, and they held a
Christmas dinner with friends. None of this, however, changed
the realities of Gerry's life. He was still grieving. The hostile, vin-
dictive reaction of others to Gerry and Randy's religious-based
commitment of love had consumed and radically changed their
lives. It also strained their relationship.

On the night of December 27, Gerry wanted to get out of the
house for a while. He called Leann Arkema hoping to talk with her.
She was not home, so he left her a message. Around ten o'clock,
Gerry went to The Apartment, the gay bar where Gerry and Randy
had first met. The bar, bedecked with holiday lights and ornaments,
had a moderate-sized crowd. Gerry took a seat at the bar. Gerry
exchanged a few words with the bartender and ordered a drink.
After a while, Gerry went the restroom. A man who recognized
him went to introduce himself. Gerry suddenly collapsed to the

floor of the bathroom and immediately lost consciousness. The man yelled for help. A nurse who was in the bar rushed in, knelt down by Gerry, and immediately began performing CPR.

"Call an ambulance!" someone yelled.

The ambulance arrived in two minutes. The nurse was still administering CPR, but Gerry did not have a pulse. The EMTs shocked his heart into activity, placed a tube in his throat to help him breath, lifted him on to the stretcher, and raced him to St. Mary's Hospital, less than a mile away.

Shortly after the ambulance left, Tim Frens walked into The Apartment. The bartender explained what had just happened. Tim immediately left and drove to two hospitals before finding the right one. When Tim arrived in the emergency waiting room, he saw Randy and Rev. Lucas. Randy stood motionless, his eyes gazing down and his shoulders slumped.

"Gerry hasn't regained consciousness," Rev. Lucas said softly. "It's very serious. It doesn't look good."

Randy asked Tim to call Marian.

On the phone Tim said, "Gerry's in the hospital. It's bad."

Marian said she'd be there right away.

"Drive carefully, we don't need another...." His voice trailed off.

When Rev. Knieriemen arrived at the hospital, she hugged Randy and together they went to the curtained area to be with Gerry. As word spread, others started to arrive. Rev. Lucas, sensing the growing anxiety in the room, ushered the friends into a private waiting room and led them in prayer. It was their shared religious beliefs, their praying together, that had brought this group of people together as friends and had sustained them.

Eventually Randy emerged from the ER. With tears trickling down his face and his voice choked with emotion, he told them Gerry had suffered a massive heart attack and was still unconscious.

He was in critical condition and was being moved to the intensive care unit.

The group walked somberly to the ICU. On their way to the elevator, Marian and Tim caught a glimpse of Gerry lying on the gurney. His body was racked with spasms.

They gathered and waited outside of the ICU. They talked about the last time each had seen Gerry, and agonized over the gut-wrenching questions: How could this happen? Why did it happen? Is there hope? There must be hope.

At Randy's request, they called other friends. The slow parade of visitors, along with the ritual of hugs, tears, and words, helped pass the time.

One hour. Two hours.

When could they see him?

Three hours.

What was going on?

Finally, a nurse summoned Randy. A small group accompanied him to Gerry's bed.

The scene was jarring. Gerry lay on a sterile hospital bed with a web of tubes and lines connecting his body to the wall of medical devices behind him. They immediately heard the rhythmic beeping of the heart monitor and the sucking sound of the ventilator pushing oxygen into Gerry's lungs. His previously vigorous body shook in convulsions, shaking the bed. Gerry's face—his beautiful, expressive face—was partially concealed by the breathing tube and mask. His skin was sweaty. His eyes were shut. He remained unconscious.

Slowly they took turns approaching Gerry, gently touching his hand, stroking his arms, and softly expressing words of hope.

Mary Banghart Therrien, a friend from AWARE, stood by his side and thought, I want to see him sit up and make one of his witty comments. We could all laugh together.[75]

Rev. Knieriemen and Rev. Lucas led the group in prayer at Gerry's bedside.

❧

On the night of Gerry's heart attack, Leann Arkema, who had agreed to be his patient advocate in case of an emergency, had been out with her family. She returned home late and checked her answering machine: "Leann, this is Gerry. I really need to talk." Because it was late, she went to bed and planned to call Gerry the next morning.

Instead, the ringing of the telephone woke her up. It was Randy calling from the hospital.

How could this be? she thought. I just heard Gerry's voice.

During her drive to the hospital, she had one recurring thought: *Why wasn't I home when he called?*

❧

When Ann Conklin walked into his hospital room the next morning, her attention was drawn to Gerry lying helpless on the stark bed. But as she took in the bigger picture, she smiled to see Gerry's high-top tennis shoes on his feet, protruding from under the sheets. Ann later learned that the shoes served a medical function of keeping the feet positioned, to prevent a condition called "foot drop," where the Achilles tendon becomes shortened and which can severely impede the patient's ability to walk. Gerry's high-tops provided a moment of levity, and to Ann they symbolized a glimmer of hope. Certainly, these smart, practical nurses would not put those awkward, oversized shoes on Gerry's feet unless they believed that he might, in fact, walk again.

It was six o'clock in the morning on December 28. Randy knew he needed to contact Gerry's parents and siblings. Gerry and his sister had lived together when Randy started dating him. Other than during that brief time, Randy had no relationship with Gerry's family other than hearing Gerry's father's voice when he telephoned to speak to Gerry. Although Randy had asked others to notify people throughout the night, he felt that he should be the one to tell Gerry's family.

Gerry's parents lived in Mount Clemens, about two and a half hours away, but Gerry's sister, Linda, lived in town. Randy phoned her first. She was devastated. Randy then contacted Gerry's parents and spoke to his father. He slowly explained the situation and ended by telling him that the doctors thought Gerry probably wouldn't come home. Gerry's father asked a few questions, thanked Randy for calling, and said they would come to the hospital. Randy also informed Gerry's brother.

That afternoon, when Gerry's parents and siblings arrived, Randy, Leann, Anne Weirich, and others were in Gerry's room. His family had brought a minister with them.

Anne Weirich had met Gerry and Randy in 1993 through Club 47 at Westminster. Gerry and Anne bonded over their shared interest in theology and had forged a deep friendship. When Anne later entered the seminary at Princeton, Gerry came to her school and spoke to a group of gay and lesbian seminarians.

Anne introduced herself to Gerry's mother and said, "Oh, I see where Gerry gets his eyes." Anne also told her how much she loved her son.

The nurses knew Gerry's story, and they respected Randy's role as Gerry's life partner, which was not the typical hospital experience for gay people at this time. With the arrival of Gerry's family, one spirited nurse stepped forward and started a conversation.

"You must be so proud of your son!" she said. She elaborated on Gerry's talents as a music teacher and said that he displayed such integrity during the Byron Center ordeal.

The nurse continued, "If I were his mother, I'd be bursting with pride."

Gerry's friends, keenly aware of the pain he had suffered because of his family's rejection, were momentarily buoyed by the nurse's comments, which addressed the proverbial elephant in the room in a manner that was polite but explicit.

After his family had some time with Gerry, Leann introduced herself. She wanted to show them love—the love that Gerry had shown her after her divorce when she was new to Westminster. She knew that his family held strong religious beliefs, so Leann told them that she was the daughter of a minister. She also told them she had worked for US Representative Vern Ehlers, a local Republican known for his conservative Christian beliefs. Leann wanted them to know that they could trust her in this difficult time. As one of Gerry's two patient advocates, Leann spent time with Gerry's family, giving them information and answering their questions.

Bruce Wilcox was relishing the Florida sunshine when he received the call from Rev. Knieriemen. He was crushed. He immediately cut short his vacation and flew home. On the plane ride to Grand Rapids, Bruce gazed out the window at the sunlit white clouds that filled Florida's blue sky. He thought of the last time he had seen Gerry.

It was a couple of days before Christmas. Randy, Gerry, and Bruce were driving back to Grand Rapids from Battle Creek. When he arrived at their house, Bruce stayed in the driver's seat while Randy and Gerry were exiting his car. At the last second something had prompted him to unbuckle his seatbelt, twist around to the back seat and hug Gerry goodbye.

Gerry's students were shattered. A couple of days after Christmas, Ryan Sekulski's mother said to him, "I have bad news about Mr. Crane." As she told him what had happened, Ryan immediately started crying. He thought of his teacher, lying unconscious in the hospital, and sat down to write a letter to Gerry.

> You have been there in my time of need; I will always be there for yours. I pray for you to awake and read this; school hasn't been the same since you left. Life wouldn't be either; I love you. I don't want anything else to happen. You have made a huge impact on my musical life. If I come up with anything on the guitar that is soothing, I think "Mr. Crane would like this." Playing drums, I play my best. I can imagine you saying, "what were you thinking?"

Ryan later gave the letter to Randy, with a note: "I regret not telling him. Not only to say thanx for being there, but teaching me how to live. Learn. Love. I love him, and I never told him."

Over the next few days, a steady stream of people came to the hospital to visit Gerry and provide solace to Randy. When Tammy Lee saw her former teacher laying helpless on the bed being kept alive by a machine, she was crushed—Gerry's warm, vibrant spirit was gone. Tammy tenderly reached for his hand, the same hand that had unexpantly grabbed her cigarette out of hers. She loved this man. Her role model. Her friend.

～⁓

The doctors told Randy that Gerry's condition had not changed. Friends created a telephone tree for the burgeoning list of people who wanted to be kept informed of Gerry's condition. They also notified people who had been out of town for the holidays. It did not take long for the media to learn about Gerry's hospitalization. His friends were intent on constructing and maintaining a wall between the media and Gerry and Randy. They worked fervently to ensure that these two men—who neither sought nor welcomed news coverage—had some degree of privacy.

The nurses and hospital staff contributed to this effort. When reporters started to appear at the hospital, staff removed Gerry's name card from the plastic plate on the wall outside of his room and from the patient list the hospital used when people telephoned to confirm a person's presence and condition at the hospital. Others spread the word for visitors to be alert for reporters. Yet this proved difficult given the large number of visitors Gerry had. When one reporter was recognized, she was instructed to immediately leave the waiting room area. Another reporter arrived carrying a new stuffed animal. Gerry's friends were outraged that she had used a gift to attempt to gain entry to his room.

On Sunday, December 29, after the morning service at Westminster Church, more than eighty people drove to the hospital to visit Gerry and Randy. The following day, hospital staff announced that visits would be limited to a smaller number of people to allow Gerry—and Randy—to rest.

By January 1, day five of the hospital vigil, many began to realize that it was unlikely that Gerry's condition would improve. The incoming calls ebbed somewhat. Telephone updates continued, however, and they often proved therapeutic for those on both sides of the call.

Randy, Leann, and Chris Gibbie, Gerry's other patient advocate, had to face the unimaginable. Leann thought back to the day Gerry had asked her to be his patient advocate: *I made him promise to live a long life.* The three of them talked to Gerry's nurses and doctors. They had many questions, and none of the responses were good.

Next, they sought an outside opinion. On New Year's Day, a neurologist from Chicago examined Gerry and conducted a battery of tests. The next day, doctors at St. Mary's Hospital ran another series. The doctors reached the same conclusion: if kept alive by artificial means, Gerry would live in a persistent vegetative state. Randy, Leann, and Chris knew what Gerry would want. Randy contacted Gerry's family to let them know that they planned to remove Gerry from life support.

On January 2, Rev. Lucas led a prayer vigil in the chapel at Westminster. The octagonal-shaped chapel had a high, conical ceiling. The wood and brick interior was accented by a large stained-glass panel. Over a hundred people attended including some of Gerry's students.

Rev. Lucas began: "We're gathered here tonight because of our deep love for Gerry Crane. We're gathered because we're shocked, troubled, and overwhelmed at the events of the last few days."

He continued with a prayer and then invited anyone who wanted to speak to approach the podium. Some people read poems, and others recounted stories of how Gerry had enriched their lives. Wendy Marty read "In Blackwater Woods," a poem written by Mary Oliver that spoke to the heartrending journey of love, loss, and letting go.

People gathered at the hospital with Randy to say goodbye and begin what they expected to be their last night with Gerry. Jackie Schoon, who had sung at the commitment ceremony, went to the hospital to be a part of the vigil. One of the nurses had previously suggested that Gerry might still be able to hear voices, so when Jackie was alone with Gerry, she gently grasped his hand and sang "On Eagle's Wings," the same song she had sung at their ceremony. His eyelids fluttered briefly. Jackie felt that he'd heard her voice—in that moment she felt at peace.

The final hours with Gerry were filled with tears and laughter, as friends shared memories and uttered their tender goodbyes. Over the course of that night, people left the room, walked the halls, and returned. They eventually all gathered around Gerry's bed, singing the songs he cherished and caressing him gently, hoping that he felt their presence and love and that it gave him a measure of peace.

When it was time to withdraw life support, the doctor turned off the monitors and delicately detached the tube connecting Gerry to the breathing machine.

Randy bent over close to Gerry and whispered, "It's okay; you can go."

Gerald Mark Crane drew his last breath at three o'clock in the morning on Friday, January 3, 1997.

Randy and the others spent the precious, holy time after Gerry died starting to settle into the reality—crying, hugging, and supporting each other, and touching Gerry's body for the last time.

Ben Boerkoel described the night as "the most sacred moment of my life."

Each person had walked an agonizing path that week. It continued as they left the hospital on that early January morning to go their separate ways. Some were enveloped in a mixture of sadness, appreciation, and peace. Others felt empty and adrift, walking into the stark darkness of winter. Each got into a cold car and drove home. The purpose and routine of their daily watch had ended. They would not return to the hospital the next day to see, touch, or talk to Gerry and be in the company of those who loved him.

A spokesperson for St. Mary's Hospital issued a press release at 9:30 am on Friday, January 3, stating that Gerry Crane had passed away, that funeral arrangements would be announced at a later time, and that the family simply asked for everyone to respect their privacy.

Before planning Gerry's memorial service, Randy needed time, time to breathe and time to move slowly around the rooms in their home—now his home—and among the things that represented their life together. He needed time to at least try to rest.

The school officials at Byron Center, however, intended otherwise.

13

Tender, True, and Brave

[Mr. Crane has] everything that is important in humanity: compassion, respect, humor, wisdom, decorum, honor, pride, vitality, strength on many levels. Mr. Crane taught me many things, not only as an educator, but as a role model, a friend and most of all, a human being.

James Morin, former student
written shortly after Gerry's death

At 10:20 a.m. on Friday, January 3—seven hours after Gerry died—David Prindle, Gerry's union representative, called Randy. He said that the school had phoned him and said they were not going to pay the rest of Gerry's severance pay. David said he was concerned that someone from the school would call Randy, and he wanted Randy to hear it from him first. A little later, Gerry's attorney, Bill Young, called Randy with the same news. The district's attorney had said that a paycheck should be arriving in Randy's mailbox and that Randy had better not try cashing it.

Randy was stunned. Gerry's death had been made public by the hospital only fifty minutes earlier and the school district had already conferred with their attorney to stop Randy from cashing a paycheck. *Where was their heart? Could it be that once they had*

*heard Gerry was hospitalized, they had discussed his severance pay,
and were waiting for him to die?*

Gerry's friends were livid about the school's attempt to stop
Randy from cashing a paycheck. Gerry had suffered at the school's
hands and had been publicly humiliated. He had been forced to
resign from a job that had brought him purpose and joy. And
now he had died, and the school's top priority was to recover a
paycheck they had mailed while Gerry was on life support? Did
they not see Randy as someone who deserved a time to mourn?

After talking with Randy, some of his friends contacted Skilling
and asked him not to attend Gerry's memorial service. Skilling
later acknowledged that he was asked not to go, but that he still
labored over the decision.

The same day Gerry died, David Prindle issued a press release
which said: "The members of the Byron Center Education Association wish to express our deepest sympathy and extend our
condolences to the family and friends of Gerry Crane. We are
stunned and saddened by this sudden and unexpected tragedy.
We offer our thoughts and prayers during this time of grief and
loss. He will be missed."

Byron Center Public Schools also issued a press release: "The
Byron Center Public Schools was saddened to hear of Gerry Crane's
death. Despite the prior public controversy, Mr. Crane's dedication
to teaching and to music was unwavering and unquestioned. He
will be missed by the many friends he made while working for
the District. The District wishes to express its condolences to Mr.
Crane's friends and family for their loss."

Randy did not have time to process the pain and anger he felt
regarding the district's demand about Gerry's paycheck; he had to

plan a service. Randy wanted to create a memorial where people who knew Gerry would recognize him in it. It would include a style and tone similar to that of their commitment ceremony; it would be religious, spiritual, dignified, and serious, but infused with humor and with plenty of music—carefully selected music.

After Gerry's death, Randy talked with Gerry's parents about the obituary. At the request of Gerry's parents, Randy left out the cities where Gerry's family lived and his brother's and sister's last names. Randy requested donations be made to The Gerald M. Crane Memorial Music Scholarship Fund. The scholarship was established to provide high school music students in west Michigan with cash awards for music lessons, workshops, summer programs, instruments, books, or other costs to pursue their musical interests during high school. Randy would be on the committee to review the applications and select the annual award recipients. Gerry's family placed an obituary in Gerry's hometown paper, *The Macomb Daily*. It did not contain information about the Grand Rapids memorial service, or Randy's name, or a request for donations to the scholarship fund.

The question of whether Byron Center Public Schools contributed to Gerry's premature death was answered, at least to some extent, by Dr. Stephen Cohle, the Kent County medical examiner who conducted an autopsy of Gerry's body. Medical examiners are charged by law to perform autopsies and investigate sudden, unexpected, accidental, and violent deaths. In that role a medical examiner is often a critical expert witness in murder cases. An experienced forensic pathologist in his late forties, Dr. Cohle lived in Byron Center with his wife, Dr. Joyce deJong, also a forensic pathologist, and their children. Dr. deJong ran for the Byron Center school board in June 1996 and lost to the candidates whose positions about Gerry's sexuality were similar to those on the then existing board.

Dr. Stephen Cohle conducted an autopsy and concluded that Gerry died of "Cardiomyopathy – Idiopathic." Cardiomyopathy is a disease of the heart muscle that makes it harder for the heart to pump blood to the rest of the body. Idiopathic means that the cause of a disease or process is not known.[76] A floppy mitral valve was listed as a significant condition contributing to, but not causing, his death. A floppy heart valve is a congenital condition that is usually not fatal. Dr. Cohle concluded that the stress of the Byron Center ordeal may have been the trigger that precipitated his fatal arrhythmia.

Dr. Cohle took heat for giving his opinion about the role that the Byron Center controversy played in Gerry's premature death. Those who harassed Gerry, drove him out of their school, and ruined his career did not want people to be able to draw that conclusion. For school officials, it was bad press. They were also concerned about civil liability. To the extent that Byron Center Public Schools contributed to Gerry's death, there could be a civil lawsuit based on negligence, also referred to as a wrongful death lawsuit. The medical examiner's professional opinion would be evidence in such a case. However Randy, as Gerry's partner in a time where Michigan did not allow gay people to get married or enter into civil unions, did not have legal standing to file a wrongful death lawsuit.

On July 1, 1997, an amended death certificate was filed and signed by another doctor. The events that led to this amendment are unclear.

The local gay community was stunned and furious with the news of Gerry's death. Many people drew a straight line from the school's treatment of Gerry beginning in 1995 to Gerry's death in January 1997. If an excellent teacher who conducted himself with dignity and restraint throughout a painful, humiliating ordeal could be publicly chastised and driven out of his job and then into an early grave, where did that leave other gay people in the community who had similarly hostile employers?

When Gerry died, The Network board talked about doing something public that would honor Gerry; they decided to place a tribute in *The Grand Rapids Press* on the day of Gerry's memorial service. They set a goal of raising enough money to purchase a half-page advertisement. A handful of people started making calls to Network supporters and found that people yearned for a way to take action to publicly honor Gerry's dignified life and help release the anger they felt now and during the prior fifteen months. The Network reached its goal within two hours.

The tribute included a photograph of Gerry and a poem written by Mary Banghart Therrien. Mary had met Gerry through AWARE and they had become good friends. She had also served as president of The Network. The poem read:

> For the lessons that you taught us,
> And the music that you made,
> For the gentle love you brought us,
> And the heavy price you paid.
>
> For integrity and courage—
> The examples that you set,
> Though you're gone, we aren't discouraged;
> Gerry Crane, we won't forget.

The tribute asked for donations to be made to the scholarship fund in Gerry's name. In general, people responded to the public tribute with words of support and donations. Some, however, sent hate mail to The Network, condemning the tribute with quotes from the Bible and blaming Gerry for his own death. A few clipped the tribute out of the newspaper, crossed out lines of verse, added their own defamatory lines, and sent it to The Network.

Gerry's memorial service was held on Tuesday, January 7, at Westminster Church at two o'clock. The media arrived early to get a sense of the space and to set up. Television cameras were not allowed inside the church, but the service was recorded on video. Twenty minutes before the service, there was a steady flow of people filling the sanctuary, exchanging sorrowful greetings and heartfelt hugs, and making their way to a seat. Since Randy had not held a visitation, this was the first time that many people had seen each other since his death.

In attendance were people from Westminster church, members of Concerned Clergy, and a large number of people from the gay community—many who were "out" but a fair number who were not. Randy's manager at Builders Square, his employer at the time, had been supportive and compassionate throughout Gerry's ordeal. He also attended the service. The founder and executive director of GLSEN, Kevin Jennings, was also there. Not only was his support meaningful for Randy, but many in the local gay community valued his presence. It demonstrated that a national organization dedicated to the well-being of gay students recognized the magnitude of Gerry's experience.

Gerry's students assumed that they would be given an excused absence for missing class to attend Gerry's funeral. This was, after all, the past practice. Skilling announced, however, that students who missed class to attend Mr. Crane's memorial service would be given an unexcused absence. Students were outraged. Instead of supporting students during their grief, the school punished them for attending Gerry's memorial. In spite of this, approximately fifty students attended his memorial. A dozen of the forty-three school staff members also attended the service. More than nine hundred people crowded into the church. Folding chairs had been added wherever there was room, and many people sat on the two sets of stairs leading to the balcony. Others stood in the church doorways, spilling out into the narthex.

Randy and a small number of close friends had arrived more than an hour before the service to gather in a private space to grieve privately, to bolster each other, to pray, and to share a meal. The past two weeks had been gut-wrenching for Randy. The best he could do was rely on his friends to help him move forward one moment at a time.

Two wooden doors at the front of the sanctuary opened. The random chatter in the pews faded as Randy appeared in the doorway, tears rolling down his face, his shoulders shaking. He walked slowly, accompanied by friends on either side and behind him, all huddled together, as if to hold him up. They all wore dark suits and somber faces. They made their way to the front row and took their seats.

Rev. Bill Evertsberg led the memorial service. Less than fifteen months earlier he had performed Gerry and Randy's commitment ceremony.

The organist, pianist, and violinist played the works of Gerry's favorite musicians, including, Beethoven, Mendelssohn, and Massenet's "Meditation from Thaïs," which had been played at their commitment ceremony.

Rev. Evertsberg's eulogy captured the feelings of most of the people in the church when he said that Gerry "died of a broken heart—figuratively and literally." He said that Gerry's homosexuality made him a better teacher because it helped him understand students who had been hurt or rejected. He said, "Maybe we'll learn family values from people who aren't supposed to have any." Referring to the 1995 movie *Mr. Holland's Opus* about a high school music teacher, Rev. Evertsberg said, "We don't need Mr. Holland; we have Mr. Crane!" [77]

He also shared a personal story about how his wife regularly tended the flower beds outside their home, and whenever Gerry drove by their house and saw her, he would roll down his window and let out a loud, razzing whistle.

The Prayers of Remembrance reflected the importance of courage to enlighten dark places and spoke to Gerry's grace and kindness:

We praise you, O God, for all those who have been tender
    and true and brave in all times and places,
for those who have enlightened the dark places of the
    earth.
Especially we thank you for your servant Gerald, the gift
    of his life,
for all in him which was good and kind and faithful and
    gentle,
for the grace with which he responded to kindness and
    unkindness alike.
We thank you that he welcomed us all with compassion.

After the memorial service, hundreds of people stayed for a reception in the large church atrium. The space has a peaceful, modern feel, with tall ceilings, plants, and an interior brick wall. A reception line to greet Randy snaked around the reception area. While waiting, many people shared stories and memories. John Chapin, who knew Gerry from AWARE, had last talked to him at Oval Beach, in Saugatuck, in the fall. They had bumped into each other and then sat together on the beach and had a long talk. John remembered that Gerry had had a deep sadness. "He didn't seem that he had any fight left in him," he reflected.

~

Prior to the memorial service, Gerry's body had been cremated. Randy had Gerry's ashes placed in an urn, to be kept in the columbarium, a wall with niches which stores cremated remains, at Westminster. He also had some of Gerry's ashes placed in an urn to keep at home. After the memorial service and reception, a group of friends gathered at Randy's house for dinner. Before they ate, Randy ceremoniously went to get the urn and placed it gingerly in the center of the dinner table. It made Gerry more present—something they all yearned for that evening.

14

Trash

Gerry Crane was an exceptional teacher and human being. He accepted me for who I was (even a terrible singer), and never told me who I was or who to be. He gave me direction in a time during my life I was aware I was "different" but didn't know how to be confident or comfortable coming to terms with who I was. He let me figure things out on my own with honest guidance and experience. He never told me how or why I was different. I can only hope I can impact someone struggling the way he did for me.

Tammy Lee
former student

Sadness. Disbelief. Anger. Urgency. These emotions permeated the local gay community after Gerry's death. There was a yearning for action. The Network was the logical place to initiate such action. The president of The Network at the time of Gerry's legal battle was Mary Banghart Therrien, who had been a supportive friend to Gerry and had written the poem for his memorial tribute in the newspaper. She had led the organization with wisdom, determination, and compassion through one of the most traumatic times for the local gay community. She was also a reporter for *Between the Lines*. Her term as president of The Network ended in December 1996 just prior to Gerry's death.

My term as president of The Network began in January 1997. Our first action was to raise money to place the half-page ad in *The*

Grand Rapids Press. Typically, raising money for a small, all-volunteer non-profit devoted to an unpopular cause was a struggle. However, raising money for Gerry, the day after his death, was easy. We split the membership list between a few of us and devoted an evening to the calls. This task actually provided a small measure of solace for those of us who made the phone calls and for those who donated. Our membership was angry, sad, and eager to contribute.

At our February and March board meetings, we discussed the need to do more. The ad was important, but raising money is a somewhat indirect, passive form of advocacy. We wanted to actively engage the community.

Like many counties, Kent County allows businesses and organizations to "adopt" a designated portion of a road and keep it clean by picking up trash a few times a year. In exchange for that commitment, the county places road signs at the beginning and end of the section, crediting the organization.

One board member said, "I looked into the Adopt-a-Road program." He paused, raised his eyebrow, and smiled. "Byron Center is available."

The other board members smiled, took it in, and then laughed. Adopting a road in Byron Center was rife with symbolism—Gerry's friends and supporters would be cleaning the trash off the streets of the town that caused him so much pain. It brought the issue back to the city that had persecuted Gerry but in a peaceful, productive manner. It was a physical activity that would bring people together, in Gerry's name. The board loved the idea.

Several years earlier, The Network had adopted a road in Ada Township, and this had drawn controversy. Twice the street signs had been vandalized: they had been ripped down, splashed with paint, and run over by a car. Now, the board needed to consider the safety of its members when they cleaned the road. Drivers might shout degrading and obscene comments from their cars. Perhaps it would get worse.

After a serious discussion, we voted on whether to move forward with adopting a road in Byron Center. The vote was unanimous to move forward.

When the Byron Center community discovered that The Network had adopted a three-mile stretch of road near downtown, many were angry and felt it was an "in-your-face" attack. From our perspective, did we and other gay people feel a sense of gratification that Byron Center residents—many who believed a gay person was an improper role model for students—would have to see the words "gay" and "lesbian" on signs firmly planted in their city every day? Absolutely. But it was much more than that. The signs and the act of adopting the road gave us the opportunity to show our support of Gerry and shine a light on the wrongful acts of the school. It served the spirit of our mission—that gay people be recognized and valued as human beings who deserve the same respect and dignity as heterosexuals. It gave people who were struggling with their own identity, especially those who lived in Byron Center and those who drove there every day, a reason for hope.

It was also intended to communicate a message to the school and those who had attacked Gerry: you treated a good man and talented teacher with contempt and disrespect. You ridiculed, humiliated, and beat down one of us. You gave other gay people, including gay students, a reason to feel afraid. In response we are making a commitment to drive to your town and pick up your trash.

For Christian members of The Network, and for those who wanted to honor Gerry's faith, it spoke to the biblical call to turn the other cheek.

This decision also reflected Gerry's spirit. He would be proud that The Network had found a creative way to draw attention to the discrimination he had faced, while also doing something good for the community of his beloved students. It was also a way to support gay people, especially gay teens, by letting them see gay adults standing tall and taking public action.

The Network had selected one of the busiest roads in Byron Center. As people drove into town, they would see our prominent Adopt-a-Road sign: "Next 3 Miles Lesbian and Gay Network," followed by a sign reading, "Welcome to Byron Center."

The county installed the signs in mid-April 1997, three months after Gerry's death. Within days, one of the signs had been spray-painted with a large red circle with a slash through it. The following week, one of the signs was removed and replaced with a bloody cow's head, suspended by a rope attached to the cow's horns. The spray painting was not surprising, but the cow's head was jarring. It evidenced sadistic rage, along with the message that gay people who participate in the clean-up should fear for their lives.

At the April board meeting we discussed whether we should move forward. We were concerned about safety on the road during the clean-up and at The Network's community center in Grand Rapids. It was not unusual to receive hate mail or telephone calls at the center, but our concerns were now heightened. We questioned how to secure our safety. The nature of the work—walking and bending down alongside a major road with a high speed limit, and with our eyes focused away from the road—made staying safe difficult. Yet the response of the board members was unanimous: we would move forward as planned.

In April, *The Grand Rapids Press* published an editorial criticizing The Network's decision to adopt the Byron Center road. The editorial spoke about the need to respect the dignity and beliefs of those who differ and argued that the passage of time would help with that process.[78] Others shared the same view. People who hold power have historically instructed those who are oppressed to "be patient" and to "give it time." They say, "Don't be so confrontational," and "People don't want to hear about it all the time." However, for those who are being oppressed, urgency is the rallying cry.

Contrary to the paper's editorial, the decision to adopt a Byron Center road led to some healing. Soon after its publication, The Network received a call from a member of the United Methodist Church of Byron Center who said that the church wanted to support us and was inviting us to a lunch at their church after our road clean-up in May. This invitation elevated our spirits and tempered our fears. It was the type of act that many gay believers, including Gerry, saw as the essence of Christianity—a calling to reach out and break bread with people who are treated poorly.

On the morning of the clean-up, our spirits were high. The sun was out, and sixty people showed up to help, including members of AWARE, Gerry's friends and students, and people from the United Methodist Church and the Pathway Ministries of Byron Center. We passed out vests, gloves, and garbage bags, and we all went to work. The traffic was consistent but not heavy; and although a few men shouted slurs from their cars, a larger number of motorists honked and gave us a "thumbs up."

Afterwards, at the United Methodist Church, their minister and people welcomed us with warmth, in a genuine spirit of love. It felt good to do meaningful work and then be welcomed and served a meal by people who lived in Byron Center. It was the perfect antidote for the pain and anger many felt. We could even imagine Gerry's warm, approving smile.

Meanwhile that spirit of love was not being modeled at Gerry's former school. The district was holding firm to their decision to prevent Randy, Gerry's legal beneficiary, from receiving the balance of the money they agreed to pay. Randy's attorney urged the district to pay the money owed—over $25,000—but to no avail.

Ever since Gerry and Randy's commitment ceremony in October 1995, Byron Center had consumed Randy's day-to-day life, and now he was grieving Gerry's death. He was exhausted. Filing a lawsuit against the school district would leave Randy vulnerable to yet more personal attacks. Gerry would not have wanted Randy to suffer more than he already had. However, Randy concluded that the school district should not get away with this injustice; he could not let them continue to take advantage of him. The school had to be stopped. He knew that the school's actions instilled fear and despondency in many gay people in the area, especially teachers and those working for homophobic employers. It was a matter of principle, and he wanted to honor Gerry's dignity. So, channeling Gerry's stubborn streak, Randy decided to fight.

Randy's attorneys sent letters to the school demanding that it pay the balance due under Gerry's settlement agreement. Again, they refused. The school's attorney compared Gerry's settlement agreement with that of a teacher who dies during the school year: since the school would not be obligated to pay the balance of the teacher's salary after death, the school had no obligation to pay the estate after Gerry's death. This is a false analogy. Teachers are paid to show up at work every day and teach. If a teacher dies during the school year, she can no longer teach. Gerry, on the other hand, was in effect being paid to resign—he had done so, and his death did not change the fact that he had resigned.

As a part of Byron Center's standard benefit package for teachers, Gerry had a life insurance policy in the amount of $20,000. After Gerry's death, the school sent Randy the appropriate forms for him to complete. Randy completed the forms, gathered a certified copy of Gerry's death certificate and other requested documents, and sent them to the insurance company, as directed. When he did not receive the proceeds, Randy called the insurance company.

The person he spoke to told Randy, "We've been instructed to tell you that you have to talk to the school board's attorney about this."

Randy discovered that as a part of the process, the school district, as the payer of the policy, was required to sign off on the payment before the insurance company would issue the check. Byron Center had decided to withhold their approval for the payment. Further, the school had the gall to tell Randy that they would agree to sign off on Gerry's life insurance payment *if* he would sign a waiver agreeing to not sue the district for the unpaid balance of Gerry's settlement payment.

For Randy, his decision was clear. He was not going to be beaten into submission by the school. In January 1999, Randy, on behalf of Gerry's estate, filed a lawsuit against the school district and its board for breach of contract. Gerry's settlement agreement required the school to pay him $43,741, in twenty-six equal installments. The purpose of the lawsuit was to require the school to pay Gerry, through his estate, approximately $25,800. One provision in the settlement agreement required Gerry to make good faith efforts to look for another job. If he found employment, the school's payments to Gerry would be reduced by the amount he earned in his new job. In response to Randy's lawsuit, the school requested that the court dismiss the lawsuit because as of January 3, 1997, when Gerry died, he had stopped making good faith efforts to look for employment. In essence, their position was that Gerry breached their agreement by dying, writing: "His unfortunate death, has, as a matter of law, terminated the agreement.... Thus, Mr. Crane's inability to seek and obtain employment after January 3, 1997 deprived the District of the benefit of its bargain."

The district absurdly argued that it was paying Gerry to search for employment and that he did not "make good-faith efforts to obtain employment" in the months after his death. Had he found comparable employment with similar health benefits, the school's argument continued, its obligation to pay Gerry would have ceased.

In March 1999, Kent County Circuit Court Judge Dennis Kolenda issued a written order denying the school's request to dismiss the case. The judge's order addressed the essence of their settlement agreement: Gerry would resign and the school would pay him money in exchange for his resignation. The judge emphatically stated that the board had enjoyed the full benefit of his resignation and that the school had avoided "the strain and acrimony of having to deal with divisive, continued demands that he be fired." The judge wrote that if the school had instead fired Gerry, they would have faced "protracted, highly visible, very expensive legal proceedings which would have inevitably been generated by the question of whether a tenured teacher can be discharged because he or she is gay." Gerry's resignation had spared them from that expense.

Therefore, Gerry's death did not justify the district's decision to stop paying the settlement amount. In fact, Judge Kolenda explained, the school benefited from Gerry's death. For example, the school no longer had to provide Gerry with health care coverage, and Gerry's death guaranteed that he would not disparage the school or apply for employment within the district—these conditions were all part of the settlement agreement. In addition, Gerry had agreed to not sue the school for discrimination, breach of contract, libel, slander, or other reasons, *and* he had waived the right of his heirs to file a lawsuit on his behalf. Had Gerry not agreed to this, it was possible that his estate would have filed such a suit.

In supporting his decision, Judge Kolenda wrote that "pledges of public faith, in particular, must be honored, unless there is a good reason to do otherwise." The judge ruled that there were no remaining issues in the case and required the school to pay Gerry's estate a lump sum of $25,800, plus interest.

Many assumed this was the end of Randy's lawsuit. Others knew better.

The school decided to appeal the decision. Before filing an appeal, the school *offered to pay one-half of the remaining contract balance to the Crane Scholarship Fund* as a full settlement of Randy's lawsuit. Randy rejected this offer.

In April 1999, the school district filed an appeal with the Michigan Court of Appeals. More than a year later, in May 2000, a three-judge panel issued a decision affirming Judge Kolenda's ruling that the school must pay Gerry's estate the balance due, $25,800, plus interest. They said the school had agreed to pay Gerry to *resign* not to look for a new job.

The school had the option to file an appeal to the Michigan Supreme Court, but it was extremely unlikely that the court would agree to hear this case.[79] The Byron Center school district finally agreed to accept the court's verdict and pay Gerry's estate the money owed—more than three years after Gerry's death.

Thank God it's over, Randy thought.

His next immediate thought was, *I hope it really is over.*

Randy went to the columbarium at Westminster. He told Gerry the news.

⁓

After the case was concluded, *The Grand Rapids Press* attempted to answer the question many were asking: How much money did it cost the taxpayers for the school to fight paying the full settlement agreement? And, earlier, how much did the school spend on attorney fees while "monitoring and investigating" Gerry for *being* a gay teacher?

The Grand Rapids Press sent the school a Freedom of Information Act request seeking billing documents and other information about the money spent on attorney fees since 1995.[80] The school responded by stating that their law firm, Varnum, did not provide them with an itemized breakdown of their work; the firm combined their time on matters relating to Gerry with other work they did for the school district.

On September 15, 2000, *The Grand Rapids Press* published an article by Ted Roelofs, who reported that officials from six of seven school districts in Kent County stated that they *would* be able to give an accounting of their legal fees related to a specific personnel matter like Gerry's. One of the six school districts was also using Varnum for their legal work.[81]

Earlier, in June 2000, Byron Center Public Schools Superintendent Swainston sent a letter to parents and community members describing the events related to Gerry, apparently in an attempt at damage control. However, the description of events in the letter was incomplete and included a cheap shot at Gerry; it said that Gerry had resigned approximately one week before band camp in 1997, implying that Gerry had left them scrambling to find a replacement to lead the camp. The letter said that in December 1995 the school considered an option which would *allow* Mr. Crane to resign, and that in August 1996, the school signed an agreement which "*allowed* Mr. Crane to immediately resign" [emphasis added]. The letter repeatedly stated that the school "declined to terminate" Gerry, but the letter did not include the school's public declaration that they would investigate and monitor Gerry because "homosexuals are not proper role models for students."

The letter said that the expenses for the lawsuit—legal work done since March 1999—was approximately $17,000 and that the school was unable to calculate attorney fees it paid before that time, adding: "It is unclear at this point, whether we are required to pay the [law] firm to research the case specific detail for media use." By framing the issue about legal requirements, the school deflected attention from the more important point—a public school should produce records showing the amount of public money they spent on a public controversy of that magnitude. If they felt justified in their actions, why not disclose the information? Did the law firm insist that they would not provide their client with an itemized billing statement, or at least an educated estimate of those fees, without billing their client for that information?

A well-informed estimate of the attorney fees could have been produced, and it was the school district's obligation to demand that their law firm produce such an estimate. The district should have insisted that the firm produce detailed billing records without charging attorney fees for gathering the information. The district was the client and it is unlikely that the law firm would risk losing the district as a client.

Large law firms have elaborate procedures which require attorneys to maintain daily calendars and detailed billing records, including telephone calls. If for some reason those records were not maintained, the firm could have put together a timeline of events. The school would have generated attorneys fee on and around the dates of: the school board meetings, the complaints which included investigations, the mailing of the anti-gay materials, the *Time* magazine article, Gerry's resignation, the arbitration, the dates between Gerry's hospitalization through the first weeks of January, and other key dates. The law firm's files would have likely included all the letters, memoranda, fax cover sheets, legal documents, and notes from conferences and telephone communications—all of which would contain dates. Telephone records would have included names such as Skilling, William Young (Gerry's attorney), news reporters, and others, along with dates that would correspond to the events on the timeline. None of this was a mystery.

In the school's failed attempt to avoid paying Gerry's estate the money it owed—$25,800—it likely incurred at least the same amount in attorney fees, costs, and interest.[82]

The Byron Center school district began their fight to rid their school of gay teachers with a righteous proclamation—gay teachers are improper role models for students. There were students in the gym that December night who knew better, some of whom had experienced heterosexual teachers, staff, and administrators, who had undermined their well-being. After Gerry died, the district dug deeper, further lowering their standards. Acting against the fragile fabric of human life, they called Randy hours after Gerry's death to tell the gay teacher's partner that he better not attempt to cash Gerry's eleven-hundred-dollar paycheck; they argued that Gerry breached his contract by dying, and the district prevented Randy from receiving Gerry's life insurance proceeds. All of this, born of their religious belief that gay teachers harm students. As it turned out the students did have poor role models at their school, but the gay teacher was not one of them.

15

Aftermath

I fear more what happens when we remain silent and let others define us. I fear what happens when we do not put a face on homosexuality. It is easy to demonize what we cannot see.... Silence leaves a void where ugliness, shame, and fear thrive.[83]

Theresa McClellan
reporter for *The Grand Rapids Press* and Gerry's friend

Gerry's story did not end with his death nor with the completion of the legal proceedings regarding his estate. Students, friends, and religious and LGBTQ+ advocacy organizations continued to be affected by his life and his death. A few of his vocal opponents thrived.

Favorite Teacher of the 1996–1997 School Year
In March 1997, Gerry Crane was voted by students as their favorite teacher of the year.

Byron Center High School Yearbook, 1997
In 1997, after Gerry died, some students at the high school wanted to create a tribute to him in the yearbook. The school administrators opposed it, even though there was precedent for including a tribute page to a student or teacher who had died during the year. Students, with the help of the yearbook teacher, defied the school's decision and surreptitiously slipped into the

yearbook a dedication page. It included a photo of Gerry, a photo of student Tammy Lee with a message she wrote about him, and a photo of student Ryan Sekulski with a poem he wrote about Gerry, titled "Stand Proud." The page was framed with phrases Gerry often said to his students: "Feet on the floor," "Deep breath," "Love ya—mean it—gotta go," "Go, girl," and a favorite: "Three words—fab. u. lous."

The yearbook pages devoted to administrators included a slogan on the top of the first page: "Serving All Who Enter Our Doors." Underneath the slogan is Principal Skilling's photograph with a quote he selected: "There is nothing more unequal, than the equal education of unequal students."

Byron Center High School Employees

Principal Bill Skilling was awarded the 1995 "Principal of the Year" award by the Michigan Association of Secondary School Principals and the Michigan Association of Student Councils and Honor Societies. Skilling continued as principal for several more years before being hired as the superintendent of Webberville Community Schools, and then superintendent of Oxford Community Schools, both in Michigan. He currently owns Reimagine Education, LCC, described as a global education awards program and elite educational forum, and works as the CEO of Michigan International Prep School, a K–12 virtual charter school.

In 1999, Brian Friddle, the high school counselor who was disciplined for denying his role in the mailing of the anti-gay book and video to parents, was promoted to assistant principal of the high school.

In 2010, Tom Hooker, a teacher at Byron Center High School who vocalized his opposition to Gerry and read Bible passages in his sex education class, was elected to Michigan's state legislature as a Republican to represent Byron Center. He was appointed vice-chair of the Education Committee and a member of the Families, Children and Seniors Committee.

Gay, Lesbian, Straight Education Network (GLSEN)

The Gay, Lesbian, Straight Education Network (GLSEN) is a national organization that serves the needs of LGBTQ+ youth. The organization was founded by Kevin Jennings, a former teacher.[84] After Gerry resigned, Jennings spent time meeting with a small group of people who wanted to start a GLSEN chapter in Kalamazoo, Michigan. The chapter was formed shortly thereafter.[85]

In the spring of 1997, GLSEN's national organization posthumously honored Gerry by naming him the recipient of their Pathfinder award, given to people who have blazed a trail to end bigotry in schools. Randy accepted the award on Gerry's behalf at the 3rd Annual Midwest conference, held in Cleveland, Ohio.

In February 1998, three of Gerry's friends—Dave Watt, who choreographed *South Pacific* at the high school, Ben Boerkoel, and Sue Olson—founded a GLSEN chapter in Grand Rapids.[86] Its founding document states that it was started "as a specific response to the harassment and subsequent death of Byron Center High School music teacher, Gerry Crane." As part of its mission, GLSEN provides an organizational structure, materials, and leadership opportunities for middle and high school students who want to form a Gay Straight Alliance (GSA) at their school. GLSEN also sponsors annual events such as No Name-Calling Week, Solidarity Week, and the Day of Silence, and provides materials and networking and leadership opportunities.

To start a GSA, a student must express an interest in doing so, talk to their principal, and find a teacher to be the group's advisor. Teachers, especially gay teachers, may not want to risk bringing that type of attention to themselves for fear of it affecting their work or even their employment. Administrators who do not want their school to have an organization with the word "gay" or similar language in its name will try to pressure the students to form a "diversity" club. Parents have also vocally opposed these clubs. As if these obstacles are not enough, the student may be subjected to bullying and rejection within their school. While the First Amendment protects the right of a student to form a GSA, many schools do not follow the law until after they have been contacted by an attorney. Many students, however, do not seek outside advocacy or even know it is an option.[87] Despite these hurdles, many students *did* initiate and continue to form GSAs in their schools.

In 2000, East Grand Rapids High School student Drew Stoppels formed the first Gay Straight Alliance (GSA) in Kent County. The following year students started GSAs at Forest Hills Central High School and Godfrey Lee High School.

During the 2008–2009 school year, Zachary DeRade, a junior, led efforts to form a GSA at Byron Center High School. He came out as gay to people at his school, talked to classmates, met with a school counselor, and met with the principal. The principal refused and told him that he could, however, start a diversity club. Though the school prevented Zachary from forming a GSA, he became involved in the local GLSEN Grand Rapids chapter and was later named to serve on GLSEN's National Student Leadership Team for the 2009–2010 school year.

The following school year Dana Morofsky and another student spoke to the principal about starting a GSA at Byron Center High School. The principal told them that there would be significant resistance and implied that they could not start the club. He made it clear that he did not want them to rock the boat. The students left the meeting frustrated and disheartened. The following school year Dana was determined to start a GSA. She talked to students, circulated a petition to form a GSA, gathered signatures and presented the petition to the principal. The principal eventually told the students that they could form a GSA if they could find a teacher to serve as the club's advisor. They talked to many teachers, all of whom either said that they were too busy or that they did not want to be associated with the club. When they asked their teacher, Christy Tripp-Arkema, however, she enthusiastically signed on. Through the courageous efforts of persistent students like Zachary and Dana, fifteen years after Gerry was forced to resign from Byron Center High School for simply being gay, the school had its first Gay Straight Alliance. While Dana had heard about Gerry from her mother, she learned more about his life from their advisor, Tripp-Arkema, who had been teaching at a local Christian school during Gerry's ordeal.

The GSA did not organize any events, such as No Name-Calling Week, in Byron Center because the students felt pressure from the administration to be secretive, and many feared being outed. What they did do, however, was meet regularly and share their experiences with each other. These exchanges were invaluable.

In 2014, Yuki DeYoung learned about Gerry during a GSA meeting at Byron Center High School. Yuki, born the year after Gerry passed away, was appalled when she heard Gerry's story and outraged that so many people in Byron Center did not know about it and that those who did know were not sharing it. She wanted to recognize Gerry's legacy.

Yuki told her art teacher, Gregory Reinstein, that she wanted to create a sculpture in memory of Gerry. Reinstein, who taught at the high school when Gerry did, attended the next GSA meeting and shared more of Gerry's story with the students.

Yuki's intent was to create a sculpture called "Cranes for Crane," which involved making a thousand origami paper cranes. According to Japanese lore, the crane was believed to live for a thousand years and was a symbol for good fortune and longevity. It developed into the belief that a person who makes a thousand paper cranes would be granted a wish. A Japanese girl who survived the bombing of Hiroshima and later died from the effect of the radiation, sought to make a thousand origami cranes.[88] The tradition of making a thousand cranes has evolved in practice to represent healing, good health, and peace. Yuki asked her classmates and others to participate by making cranes for the sculpture. Her wish—that Byron Center High School would be a safe space for its LGBTQ+ students and staff. Unable to generate enough interest in it, she decided to create a mixed media piece that included origami cranes. It was displayed in the art room so other students would learn about Gerry's life.

Related School Issues

In April 2015, the Michigan Association of Civil Rights Activists charged that Byron Center Public Schools raised religious entanglement issues with their Student Life and Leadership class at the high school because the class had engaged in a fundraising project for Operation Christmas Child, a program developed by Samaritan's Purse, an international evangelical Christian relief organization.

In May 2015, after receiving a complaint from a Bryon Center parent, the Michigan Association of Civil Rights Activists complained that Byron Center Public Schools organized and supported a baccalaureate service, which is a religious service, for graduating seniors. The school promoted the event on its district website and on its outdoor electric school sign.

Media

In January 1998, journalist Deborah Roberts interviewed people in Byron Center for a story about Gerry, to be aired on ABC's show *20/20*, co-hosted by Barbara Walters and Hugh Downs. Roberts interviewed Randy, Rev. Richard Gregory, several of Gerry's former students, parents of former students, and GLSEN's executive director, Kevin Jennings. For the interviews with former students, Roberts met with them at Cappuccino Jo's, a local coffeehouse where Gerry used to meet with students.

The feature, "Please Don't Teach Our Kids," aired on March 13, 1998. It also included a story about a Utah high school psychology teacher and girls' volleyball coach, Wendy Weaver. She was a respected teacher and had been named Utah's 1995 Coach of the Year. After parents discovered that she was in a lesbian relationship, she was fired from her coaching position and directed to not talk about her sexual orientation in school or in the community.

Westminster Presbyterian Church

Rev. Bill Evertsberg was in his early forties at the time of the conflict and was raising a family. This public controversy engulfed him. People said cruel things about him; he received nasty notes; a few friends told him that he was going to hell; some members said, behind his back, that they wanted him to resign; and he was vilified by many in the local Christian community outside of his church.

In April 1997, Rev. Evertsberg left Westminster Presbyterian and accepted a call to First Presbyterian Church in Greenwich, Connecticut. He had originally accepted the call in December 1996, but it was not announced until later. Rev. Evertsberg said that his decision to leave Westminster was not based on the reaction to his participation in Gerry and Randy's commitment ceremony. "It was time," he said. He had been at Westminster for seven years, and it is not unusual for ministers to move to a different congregation after that period of time. Rev. Evertsberg never wavered from his belief that he was serving the will of God. In assessing his decision to officiate the commitment ceremony, he said, "I never questioned my decision. I'm glad I did it. I'm proud. We fought a small battle in a big fight—advanced the cause."

Significantly, after Rev. Evertsberg left Westminster, the church leadership continued to move forward on this issue. In September 2009, for the first time, Westminster held a commitment ceremony for a gay couple in the sanctuary. It was performed by Rev. Anne Weirich, Gerry's friend, along with Rev. Chandler Stokes, Westminster's minister.

In 2011, the Presbyterian Church (USA) approved the ordination and installation of openly-gay people who are in a same-sex relationship as ministers, elders, and deacons. In 2014, it permitted ministers to conduct same-sex marriage ceremonies in states where it was permitted by law.

Rev. Jim Lucas

In September 1997, Rev. Jim Lucas, the gay Christian Reformed minister who led Gerry and others at AWARE, expressed his view that "faithful, committed, permanent, same-sex unions can be an experience of God's grace and within God's will for those who find they are not able to maintain a life of celibacy." Shortly after, AWARE publicly issued a similar statement. These statements caused a firestorm within the Christian Reformed Church. In May 1998, six years after Rev. Lucas gave his speech at Calvin College titled, "What Would You Say If You Knew I Was Gay?" the Christian Reformed Church revoked Rev. Lucas's ordination. Some church officials described the decision to revoke Rev. Lucas's ordination as merely procedural—that the decision was made based on the fact that he had not received a call for nine years. Of course, he did not get a call because of his sexual orientation.

In 2001, Rev. Lucas founded GIFT (Gays In Faith Together), an organization that seeks to affirm LGBTQ+ people of faith and end spiritual harm against LGBTQ+ people.[89] In addition to his work as chaplain for GIFT, Rev. Lucas works as a hospital chaplain.

Concerned Clergy

Concerned Clergy continued its work. On January 18, 1997, only two weeks after Gerry's death, they sponsored an all-day conference, "Embracing Our Family: What the Bible Really Says about Homosexuality." The event, which had been in the works for months, was dedicated to Gerry. The program read: "His faith, courage, and integrity inspired us, as clergy, to come together and give voice to our heartfelt beliefs." The conference, which was held at Trinity United Methodist Church, featured internationally known biblical scholar and author Dr. Robin Scroggs. Over one hundred people attended the conference. In addition to clergy, the event featured facilitators from within the local LGBTQ+ community including The Network, PFLAG, AWARE, Dignity (Catholic), and Windfire, a LGBTQ+ youth group.[90] On March 14, 1998, Concerned Clergy held another event, "Same-Sex Couples: Equal Rights and Equal Rites." It featured Dr. Virginia Ramey Mollenkott, a writer and professor specializing in feminist theology and lesbian, gay, bisexual, and transgender theology.

Concerned Clergy also commissioned a play, *Come in from the Rain*, written by Mike Smolinski and co-directed by Fred Sebulske and Greg Stroh, which explores how homosexuality and homophobia impact a church.[91] The story involves a gay-bashing incident in a coffee shop, witnessed by a minister. The perpetrator attends the minister's church. The story is meant to show "how our actions or inaction affect everyone around us and how homophobia hurts not only the victim and the aggressor but also everyone with whom these people come in contact ... and even those who just hear about it."[92] The play was produced in 2000, and all four performances were sold out.

Many Protestant churches use a specific phrase, unique to their denomination, to communicate that they are "gay friendly." For example, Presbyterians use the term "More Light," Methodists use

"Welcoming," and the United Church of Christ uses "Open and Affirming." The decision to adopt a gay-friendly status is decided at the congregational level, after members engage in a process of discussion and discernment. In 1998, Plymouth United Church of Christ, where Rev. Doug Van Doren ministered, became "Open and Affirming." In 2002, East Congregational Church became "Open and Affirming." By 2004, twenty-two churches in Kent County self-identified as gay friendly.

Friends

Leann Arkema

Gerry's death rattled Leann to her core. His death made her question many things. Her work for a congressman no longer made sense to her. In 1998, she accepted the position of president and CEO of Gilda's Club Grand Rapids. Named after the late comedian Gilda Radner, it is a national organization that provides social and emotional support for people living with cancer, cancer survivors, and their families. Leann describes the essence of her career change in one telling sentence, "I went into the grief and loss business."

Marian Vanderwall

In March 1998, Marian Vanderwall gave birth to a son. Before she became pregnant, Gerry had agreed to be her birth coach and had looked forward to playing the important role of Uncle Gerry. Marian has woven Gerry's spirit into her son's life with her stories and through his name: Samuel Benton Crane Vanderwall.

Theresa McClellan

Theresa McClellan, a reporter for *The Grand Rapids Press*, was a good friend of Gerry's. Because of their friendship, she could not report on his story. It was painful for her to witness the way he was treated. In the months after his death, Theresa gave more thought to her own journey as a thirty-nine-year-old African American Christian living as a lesbian in Grand Rapids.

In April 1997, when actor Ellen DeGeneres came out as gay, as did her character on the *Ellen* show, the editors at the *Press* discussed including the coming out story of one or more lesbians who lived in the Grand Rapids area.[93] Theresa decided that this was an appropriate time for her to come out professionally, and she wrote her own story. She had been a reporter with the *Press* for seventeen years, and publicly coming out could have derailed her career. However, Gerry's story, including his death, emboldened her to take this step.

Students

Tammy Lee

After seeing Gerry mistreated by the school district, Tammy Lee, who is gay, concluded that it was not safe for her to pursue a teaching career. The actions of the Byron Center school district not only hurt Tammy but also deprived future generations of having her for a teacher.

On January 3, 2002, the fifth anniversary of Gerry's death, Tammy placed a memorial in *The Grand Rapids Press*. It read:

For my best friend who passed away.
Five years ago on this date.
You were a man of great courage and of unconditional strength.
You are my inspiration even to this day.
To the best teacher a girl could ever have.

Mr. Crane, you are missed.

Inspired Always

Love,

Tammy Lee

In 2011, at age thirty-two—Gerry's age at the time of his death—Tammy Lee got a tattoo as a tribute to her former choir teacher. She selected lines from a song they had sung in choir, "Colors of the Wind," from the Disney movie *Pocahontas*. The tattoo, on her left arm, consists of the lyrics and musical notes of four lines from the song.

Whenever someone asks about her tattoo, she tells them about Gerry. "I believe these words are about him and what he stood for. He set an example for many people. I still get goosebumps thinking about him."

Charlie Comero

Another choir student, Charlie Comero, was in was in the 10th grade during Gerry's last year of teaching. In 2010, thirteen years after graduating from high school, Charlie sent this email to Principal Skilling:

Dr. Skilling,

This is NOT a hate letter—please take 30 seconds and read.

...It doesn't bother me that we might not have the same religious beliefs, but what bothers me is how you felt your beliefs were righteous—even at the expense of so many people who were gay at Byron Center High School. It was a horrible time for everyone—and I am simply writing this letter to encourage you to learn from the experience. Such complacency, when you have such a political pull, is abuse. This, then, speaks volumes to the action you did take during 1996–1997.

You hurt me. You hurt a lot of people—and you should know that. You were supposed to be my principal—someone I could trust, look up to, admire.

...I am writing you not out of hate, but out of concern. I encourage you to start a GSA in Oxford [Community Schools] (Heck, I challenge you). I encourage you to be human and humane to others. I hope, looking back, you see that what you were doing was anything but love. Justifying hatred with love allows you to not have guilt when your actions hurt so many—and I can't think of a better definition for "cowardly."

Dr. Skilling, I almost killed myself as a teenager during these years. This is not because of you, but because there were no positive resources for me to go to. Please consider my challenge.

If I may, I am now owner and executive officer of a very successful company—and I have a beautiful, big family...

All the best,

Skilling never replied.

More recently, Charlie made national news as an advocate for transgender rights. In 2016, North Carolina passed an anti-LGBTQ+ law banning local laws that protect LGBTQ+ people from discrimination. The law, referred to as HB2, also prohibited transgender people from using bathrooms and locker rooms that align with their gender identity. Charlie, a transgender male, created cards to hand out to people who questioned his presence in a bathroom designated for women. The card read: "My name is Charlie. I'm following the law that was passed on March 23rd. I am a transgender man who would rather be using the men's room right now. This is likely uncomfortable for both of us. Please contact your legislature and tell them you oppose HB2." After using the cards Charlie came to realize that some people do not understand what it means to be a transgender male. Charlie changed the card by adding, "A transgender male is someone whose birth certificate (at the time of birth) says female and that is not how I live my everyday life." In 2019, a federal court signed a consent decree which allows transgender people to use public facilities consistent with their gender identity.

Randy Block

In 1998, Randy traveled throughout the country telling Gerry's story at fundraising events for Lambda Legal. He often attended the events with Margarethe Cammermeyer, who after serving for twenty-five years in the military, was discharged for being lesbian.[94]

Randy could have filed a lawsuit against Byron Center Public Schools to collect Gerry's life insurance proceeds. He decided not to do so. Gerry died one month after fighting for his legal rights in an arbitration hearing—a process which required him to relive in painful detail the events of the prior year. Randy needed to cut his interactions with Byron Center Public Schools. His health required it.

Conclusion

Gerry Crane's teaching career was destroyed because he was gay. Gerry's students and well over a generation of students lost the opportunity to benefit from his talents as an educator. Over the past twenty-five years, LGBTQ+ teachers have continued to experience discrimination and to work in fear of reprisal for being "out" or, as in Gerry's case, for being "outed" by someone else.

Religion and the First Amendment

Gerry's case illustrates the limits of applying "community standards" in public education. Even though public education is primarily regulated by state and local governments, school boards cannot base decisions on community standards if the application of those standards violate constitutional law. Neither can local community standards be used as a guise to promote a religious agenda.

Byron Center High School routinely blurred the lines between a public school education and a Christian school education. Principal Skilling's decision to bring Peter Marshall to the school to speak about Christianity, American history, and homosexuality, at the same time parents were pulling their children out of Gerry's classes and immediately before critical school board meetings, connected the school's treatment of Gerry to a particular religious perspective. The school also crossed the boundary of the separation of church and state in multiple other ways: by allowing a teacher to read from the Bible during health class; by allowing the principal to prominently display the Bible in his office; and by telling a student that she was a sinner if she continued to express her support for her gay teacher.

Gerry's existence as a gay man, and his decision to exchange vows of commitment with a man, did not interfere with the rights of students, parents, or other residents to freely exercise their religion. Parents were free to continue to practice their religion and teach their convictions to their children. The more appropriate question was: to what extent did the school violate Gerry's right to exercise *his* religious beliefs? Ironically Christians, including the school officials, were attacking Gerry for exercising his Christian faith. The officiant at Gerry's commitment ceremony was a Presbyterian minister, and the ceremony consisted of Christian readings, prayers, and music—all of which was evident from the program that school officials had in their possession.

Christian churches had, and still have, theological differences about homosexuality. In west Michigan this was evident from various letters sent to the school, published in newspapers, and from the work of Concerned Clergy. Those who wanted Gerry fired were in effect demanding that the school board make personnel decisions based on theological tenets followed by their church and, by implication, favor their doctrine over other Christian theology. The freedom to exercise religion does not include the right to have one's children be taught by public school teachers who share one's faith or to demand that a public school teacher be fired for exercising his religious rights. Millions of people throughout the country hold religious convictions, and others are agnostic and atheist, yet most of these people do not demand that their beliefs be adopted by their children's public school teachers.

Proper Role Model

While the school characterized Gerry as being an improper role model, his actions said otherwise. In the midst of constant attacks, harassment, humiliation, disciplinary meetings, and media coverage, Gerry remained focused on his work, producing stellar choir and band performances. For eight months, Gerry had to defend himself against thirteen formal complaints, all of which were eventually dropped—two after arbitration. While his classes were being gutted and his sexual orientation was being discussed in a series of public school board meetings, Gerry delivered outstanding choir and band performances. Instead of pulling back on his commitment to his students, Gerry devoted extra work hours after school, in the evening, and on weekends to his students: he led students in a Saturday band competition where they won "Best Band," and he directed a successful production of *South Pacific* during this time. The school not only failed to applaud his dedication, they also disciplined him for using Rodgers and Hammerstein songs and Disney songs—the age-appropriate, mainstream music used in high schools across the country. He modeled resilience, determination, commitment, strength of character, compassion, and focus.

As early as February 1996, Gerry felt the school was engaged in a "witch hunt" that would "end with a lynching—if not in reality, then most certainly in spirit." When Gerry resigned in July 1996, he explained that his humanity was at stake. None of this was hyperbole. The school crushed his spirit. The school broke his heart.

In light of the facts, the question should have been whether the school's leaders, specifically, the trustees, Principal Skilling, and Superintendent Swainston, were proper role models for the students. Was it in the best interest of the students to break the spirit of one of their best teachers, who in the school's own assessment, maintained high expectations for himself and his students and raised the standard of its music program? Of course, it was not.

The Question of Decency

Was this a case where a school's leadership was simply not up to the task of managing a public controversy of this magnitude? Or did they act in a way that was unjustifiable and even lacking in decency? The clearest assessment of this question can be seen in the school's actions *after* it forced Gerry to resign.

Compassionate administrators would have honored the students' loss by reassuring them that they would be given an excused absence if they attended his memorial service. Instead they penalized students for attending their former teacher's memorial service. Compassionate administrators would have encouraged students to create a tribute to their teacher in their school yearbook. Did they believe that a deceased exemplary teacher should not be honored because of his sexuality? Even if that was their thinking, they should have wanted to provide his students a healthy way of working through their grief.

Compassionate school leaders would have respected Gerry's partner, Randy, and had the decency to give him time to mourn in the hours after Gerry's death, regardless of their religious views of homosexuality. Compassionate school officials would not have been preoccupied with attempting to intercept Gerry's most recent paycheck hours after his death.

Compassionate school officials would have viewed Gerry's death as something more than a financial opportunity for the school. They would have continued to send Gerry's settlement payments and would have promptly completed the paperwork needed to facilitate the payment of Gerry's life insurance proceeds.

None of these things occurred.

Byron Center Public Schools' Legacy

Byron Center Public Schools played an instrumental role in creating the initial problem Gerry faced and fueling the controversy. The district bears responsibility for causing Gerry deep pain, destroying his career, and likely contributing to his early death. It also failed to meet the needs of its students, especially those students who did not share the dominant religious beliefs of the trustees and top administrators.

This is a part of the school district's history. Faced with this history, the school should examine this past and decide if it reflects the district's current values. If it does not, the district should take action that demonstrates its changed values.

First, the school board should pass a resolution acknowledging the damage it caused and apologizing to its students, to Randy, to Gerry's other loved ones and friends, and to LGBTQ+ people who were hurt by its actions. Second, they should organize a meaningful event honoring Gerry Crane's legacy and attempt to make amends with former students who were hurt by the school. To that end, the event must be based on input from former students, parents, and others who knew and supported Gerry. It would be important to include a forum for students and others who were hurt by the school's actions to tell their story. Third, they should form an advisory board that includes LGBTQ+ students, and students and parents who advocated on Gerry's behalf at that time. It should also include LGBTQ+ teachers and allies. The advisory board's charge should include obtaining input from organizations such as GLSEN and local LGBTQ+ groups about creating safe, affirming school environments for its students, teachers, and staff, conducting a climate survey, and making additional recommendations to the school board.

None of these measures will make up for the damage done, but they would provide an opportunity for the district to set itself apart from its past. They would facilitate crucial change and generate meaningful dialogue, and in doing so, serve the best interest of current and future LGBTQ+ and LGBTQ+ supportive students, teachers, staff, parents, and many others.

Concerned Clergy and Religious Affirmation

For LGBTQ+ people to be raised in a faith tradition that condemns homosexuality and that excludes LGBTQ+ people from eternal life is devastating, both spiritually and psychologically. Individuals who carry these religious beliefs into adulthood are left to choose between coming out and accepting eternal damnation or living a repressed life steeped in torment, self-hate, and deceit. The pain, anger, and grief involved in this decision is often magnified by family coercion and rejection.

Concerned Clergy sought to change that narrative for others. As they heard the way Christianity was being used to demonize Gerry, this group of ministers came together to educate and raise awareness of the theology and history that supports their own Christian-based perspective. Concerned Clergy created lasting change, and offered love and hope to many LGBTQ+ people, including students, who witnessed the public persecution of a man based solely on his sexual orientation.

Gerry Crane's Legacy

Gerry's story is not only about a community of people who lived in a particular zip code during the mid-1990s. Such a rendition furthers the human tendency to blame others for the problems of the day. This type of packaging also prevents people from honestly assessing the climate in their own community, and from examining how their own actions and inaction perpetuates homophobia and transphobia today.

Teachers throughout the nation continue to live partially or totally closeted lives to maintain their employment. Teachers who are closeted—and many who are out—remain concerned that their sexuality or gender identity will negatively affect their employment. Homophobic and transphobic parents, teachers, staff, administrators, and board trustees still exist. Laws provide incentives for schools and other employers to do better and create an avenue for those wronged to seek redress, but laws do not end discrimination.

The social and legal debates surrounding the interpretation of the Establishment Clause in the First Amendment—the separation of church and state—served as bookends of Gerry's life. As a senior in high school he struggled with how to discuss religious doctrine in a public school course about literature and the Bible. Ironically, like an avalanche, the anti-gay religious and social doctrine of his youth, which had brought him to the brink of death in his college years, and which he had set aside in favor of a more affirming and inclusive theological tradition, cascaded back into his life a decade later, destroying his career, and arguably, his life.

Gerry was raised with this type of belief system and he lived his life in a society steeped in homophobia. He wrestled the demons born of his religious upbringing and education. He had not only survived but carved out an authentic life filled with love, meaning, and a community of Christians who valued his worth as a human being. He formed friendships with people who, like him, had reached the conclusion that they could not deny or suppress their sexuality, and who wanted to reconcile their faith with their sexuality.

As a teacher, Gerry modeled excellence. He was a disciplinarian with high expectations who tempered his serious side with heart and humor. He inspired students to do better and to believe in themselves. The pain and struggles he endured throughout his life underscored his capacity for empathy. Students brought him their concerns and problems, and they left those encounters feeling better. He was dedicated to and energized by his students, and he channeled that energy back into his teaching.

Gerry dared to believe that his professional relationships—with parents, colleagues, and school officials—along with his exceptional work and his dedication to the school's music program would carry the day, that enough people would get angry, come together on his behalf, and make a difference. This ultimately did not happen. In spite of that, Gerry remained a role model for grace, dignity, and courage under fire. Gerry continues to teach and inspire others through his life story.

Appendix A

Signatories
Pastoral Letter from Concerned Clergy in
West Michigan

An asterisk (*) indicates the 32 signers of the original letter published in The Grand Rapids Press *on June 2, 1996. Those who signed the letter provided the denominational affiliations, church relations, and titles indicated below, stating that they were speaking to their churches but not necessarily for them. Ultimately, additional clergy signed on to the letter as indicated below.*

Presbyterian Church (USA)
*William Evertsberg, Westminster
*Linda Knieriemen, Westminster
*Robert Bos, Spiritual Care Counselor, Grand Rapids Hospice
Joseph W. Hill
Riley Jensen
Thomas R. Nelson

United Church of Christ
*Brian Byrne, East Congregational UCC
*Ted Eisenheimer, Second Congregational UCC
*David Reese, Associate Conference Minister
*Richard Rowlands, Smith Memorial Congregational UCC
*Ronald Skidmore, South Congregational UCC
*David Lee Smith, Burlingame Congregational UCC
*Janice Thorsen, Second Congregational UCC
*Douglas Van Doren, Plymouth UCC
*Judith Whitwer, Therapist, The Marriage and Family Center Inc.
*Ken Whitwer, Interim Ministry Specialist

Sarah Campbell
Pamela Doty-Nation
Kenneth Gottman
George Heartwell
Al Mascia
Marc Ian Stewart
Eric Thorsen
Keith Titus

Fountain Street Church (Non-Denominational)
*Donald Hoekstra
*David Rankin
*Sue Sinnamon

Universal Fellowship of Metropolitan Community Churches
*Linda Stoner, Reconciliation MCC
*Carole Hoke, Lighthouse of Hope MCC
Dan Bennett

United Methodist Church
*Ellen Brubaker, Aldersgate UMC
*Kim Gladding, Faith UMC
*Gary Haller, First UMC
*Deborah Johnson, Hudsonville UMC
*Chris Lane, Genesis UMC
*Jane Lippert, Genesis UMC
*Barry Petrucci, United Methodist Metropolitan Ministry
*Gerald Pohly, Trinity UMC
*Gerald Toshalis, Trinity UMC
Don Entenman
A. Edward Perkins
Marge Rivera

Robert Smith

The Episcopal Church
*Michael Fedewa, St. Andrew's Episcopal Churh
Jennifer Adams
Valerie Ambrose
John Crean
William J. Fleener
Kathleen Kingslight
Barbara Panarites
John Panarites
Joanne Parkhurst
William G. Smith, III
William H. Smith
Tom Toeller-Novak

Christ Community Church, Spring Lake (Non-Denominational)
*Colette Volkema DeNooyer
*John (Bob) Kleinheksel, Jr.
*Richard Rhem
*Peter Theune

Additional Signatories
Andrew De Braber, RCA
Nat Carter, Unity Church
David Neven, Coptic Christian Fellowship

Appendix B

Resources

Organizations

American Civil Liberties Union (ACLU)	www.aclu.org
Campus Pride	www.campuspride.org
Colage (Children of LGBT Parents)	www.colage.org
Faith Based Resources	www.strongfamilyalliance.org
	www.pbs.org/independentlens/content/ love-free-or-die_lgbt
Federation of LGBTQ Asian American, South Asian, Southeast Asian and Pacific Islander Organizations	www.nqapia.org
GLAAD	www.glaad.org
GLSEN	www.glsen.org
Human Rights Campaign	www.hrc.org
International LGBTI Association	ilga.org
Lambda Legal	www.lambdalegal.org
Latino Equality Alliance	www.latinoequalityalliance.org/ our-work
Matthew Shepard Foundation	www.matthewshepard.org
National Black Justice Coalition	www.nbjc.org
National Center for Lesbian Rights	www.nclrights.org
National Center for Transgender Equality	transequality.org

National LGBTQ Task Force	www.thetaskforce.org
PFLAG	pflag.org
SAGE (LGBT Elders)	www.sageusa.org
Soulforce (Sabotage Christian Supremacy)	www.soulforce.org
Strong Family Alliance	www.strongfamilyalliance.org
Transgender Law Center	transgenderlawcenter.org
The Trevor Project	www.thetrevorproject.org
Crisis Intervention/ Suicide Prevention	www.thetrevorproject.org/get-help-now
Trevor Lifeline	1.866.488.7386

Books

Catherine Connell, *School's Out: Gay and Lesbian Teachers in the Classroom*, University of California Press (2015).

Kevin Jennings, *Mama's Boy, Preacher's Son: A Memoir of Growing up, Coming Out, and Changing America's Schools*, Beacon Press (2006).

Kevin Jennings, *One Teacher in Ten in the New Millennium: LGBT Educators Speak Out About What's Gotten Better ... and What Hasn't*, Beacon Press (2015).

Mel White, *Stranger at the Gate: To Be Gay and Christian in America*, Simon & Schuster (2015); originally published by Plume (1995).

Endnotes

1. Formed in 1987, the Lesbian, Gay and Bisexual Community Network of West Michigan, referred to as "The Network," was the largest organization of its type in west Michigan.

2. LGBTQ+ is an acronym that refers to individuals who are lesbian, gay, bisexual, transgender, or queer. The plus symbol refers to other sexual orientations and gender identities including questioning, intersex, Two-Spirit, pansexual, androgynous, and asexual. Intersex refers to a person born with reproductive or sexual anatomy that is not completely male or female. Two-Spirit is used by some Indigenous people to describe a person who identifies as having both a male and female essence or spirit. Pansexual refers to a person who has the potential for emotional, romantic, or sexual attraction towards persons of all gender identities and biological sexes.

3. *Bowers v. Hardwick*, 478 U.S. 186 (1986).

4. *Lawrence v. Texas*, 539 U.S. 558 (2003).

5. *United States v. Windsor*, 570 U.S. 744 (2013).

6. *Obergefell v. Hodges*, 576 U.S. 644 (2015).

7. *Bostock v. Clayton County*, 590 U.S. ___ (2020).

8. Homophobia refers to the fear and hatred of or discomfort with people who are attracted to people of the same sex. Transphobia refers to the fear and hatred of or discomfort with transgender people.

9. In addition to the four public board meetings, the school board held a working meeting about Gerry Crane on December 11, 1995, which was closed to the public.

10. Byron Center and Grand Rapids are in Kent County. Locally, the term "west Michigan" is often used to include four counties: Allegan, Kent, Muskegon, and Ottawa. The author's use of the term "west Michigan" in this book refers to those counties. One aspect of west

Michigan's culture is a large, religiously and politicly conservative population.

11. It is a misnomer to say that a couple becomes "married" during a commitment ceremony, which by definition, does not carry any legal significance.

12. This number includes hundreds of letters which were received after the December 18, 1995, school board meeting.

13. Letter to Superintendent Swainston, school board, and faculty, by Barbara Colby, November 20, 1995.

14. The school district's law firm, Varnum, was named Varnum, Riddering, Schmidt and Howlett at the time.

15. Mary Banghart Therrien, "Don't take away our teacher," *Between the Lines*, January 1996, p. 26.

16. Peg West, "Decision brings confusion, anger, joy," *The Grand Rapids Press*, December 19, 1995, p. A4.

17. Joanne Voorhees later served as a Republican legislator in the Michigan House of Representatives from 1998 to 2004.

Phyllis Schlafly was an anti-gay, anti-feminist, conservative activist who founded the Eagle Forum in 1972. She opposed and helped to defeat the Equal Rights Amendment, a constitutional amendment that states that women have the same rights as men under the law. A large part of her strategy to defeat the ERA was to attack lesbians, gay men, and homosexuality.

18. Ruth Butler, "Real threats to kids aren't from gay teacher," *The Grand Rapids Press*, December 6, 1995.

19. The Church of the Nazarene and The Wesleyan Church both emerged out of the nineteenth century Holiness Movement, a period characterized by the rise of evangelistic revival meetings. Ministers in the Church of the Nazarene, the Wesleyan Church, and the Baptist Church considered homosexuality sinful and a sexual perversion, and preached that the homosexual would suffer the wrath of God.

20. For more information about the movie industry's treatment of homosexuality, see Vito Russo, *The Celluloid Closet: Homosexuality in the Movies* (New York: Harper & Row, 1981; revised ed. 1987) or the

documentary film based on the book, *The Celluloid Closet*, directed by Rob Epstein and Jeffrey Friedman, narrated by Lily Tomlin (1995).

21. *McLean v. Arkansas Board of Education*, 529 F. Supp. 1255 (ED Ark. 1982).

22. On January 1, 1802, President Jefferson, in a letter to the Danbury Baptist Association, wrote:

> Believing with you that religion is a matter which lies solely between Man & his God, that he owes account to none other for his faith or his worship, that the legitimate powers of government reach actions only, & not opinions, I contemplate with sovereign reverence that act of the whole American people which declared that their legislature should "make no law respecting an establishment of religion, or prohibiting the free exercise thereof," thus building a wall of separation between Church & State.

See https://www.au.org/sites/default/files/pdf_documents/jeffersons-letter-to-the.pdf.

23. Eileen White, "President Reagan Backs Constitutional Change On Prayer in School," *Education Week*, May 12, 1982, https://www.edweek.org/ew/articles/1982/05/12/02250033.h01.html.

24. Southern Baptist Convention 1982 Resolutions 9 and 14. https://www.sbc.net/resource-library/resolutions/resolution-on-prayer-in-schools.

25. Thirty-five years after Reagan adopted the campaign slogan "Let's Make America Great Again," Donald Trump announced his candidacy for president using the slogan "Make America Great Again," which again resonated with people yearning for a return to the cultural and political climate of an earlier time, which many identified as being the 1950s.

26. In 1994, the college changed its name to Cornerstone College and Grand Rapids Baptist Seminary, and then became Cornerstone University in 1999.

27. Prof. John Varineau, letter of recommendation, 1985.

28. Two Reformed Protestant denominations, the Reformed Church in America (RCA) and the Christian Reformed Church (CRC), have

contributed significantly to the religious and cultural identity of west Michigan.

The first Dutch Reformed congregation in the United States was organized in 1628 by immigrants from the Netherlands who settled in New Amsterdam (now New York City). Over two centuries the church in America grew in numbers and also became increasingly autonomous from the home church in the Netherlands, formally adopting a constitution in 1792 and the name of the Reformed Church in America in 1867.

The nineteenth century saw the church expand westward into the Midwest, with the founding of Hope College and Western Theological Seminary in west Michigan at the mid-century. This period also was one of increased Dutch immigration to the region and ultimately denominational schism, with 1857 marking the secession in west Michigan of a more theologically conservative group of congregants who formed the Christian Reformed Church in North America (CRC) at that time.

Calvin College and Calvin Theological Seminary in Grand Rapids were both founded by the CRC in this period. Leaders of the CRC at the time—and today—highly value confessional identity and doctrinal purity. Hope College, located in Holland, Michigan, and founded in 1862, is affiliated with the RCA. The US headquarters of the CRC is located in Grand Rapids, as is one of the national denominational offices of the RCA. Both denominations, the RCA and the CRC, continue to have strong ties and influence in west Michigan.

29. Gerry Crane's teacher evaluation, Calvin College music professor, Dr. Dale Topp, May 16, 1986.

30. Gerry Crane's teacher recommendation, Jackson Park Junior High principal, Wyoming Public Schools, Jerry R. Thornton, 1992.

31. Gerry Crane's teacher recommendation, Rogers High School musical director, Wyoming Public Schools, Eleanor Keur, 1992.

32. As a port town in the mid-1800s, the area saw a steady flow of mill workers and sailors. The use of Oval Beach for nude sunbathing can be dated back to at least the late 1890s. See the Saugatuck Douglas Historical Society, The Gay History Project. http://sdhistoricalsociety.org/projects/gay_history.php.

33. Rev. Jim Lucas's talk, prepared on May 12, 1992.

34. In 1973, the American Psychiatric Association declared that homosexuality is not a mental illness.

35. The organizations include: the American Medical Association, the American Psychiatric Association, the American Psychological Association, the American Academy of Child and Adolescent Psychiatry, and the National Association of Social Workers.

36. The states which prohibit conversion therapy for minors are: California, Colorado, Connecticut, Delaware, Hawaii, Illinois, Maine, Maryland, Massachusetts, Nevada, New Hampshire, New Jersey, New Mexico, New York, Oregon, Rhode Island, Utah, Vermont, Virginia, and Washington.

37. Joseph Nicolosi, *Reparative Therapy of Male Homosexuality*, Northvale, NJ: Jason Aronson, 1991.

38. The national Dignity organization was formed a couple of months before Stonewall, an uprising in New York that marks the beginning of the modern gay rights movement. While Dignity USA is still operating, the Grand Rapids chapter disbanded in or around 2000.

39. AWARE groups were formed in Grand Rapids and London, Ontario, in 1991, and in Burbank, California, in 1995.

40. Diane McElfish was the violinist, and David Cogswell the pianist.

41. John Calvi, a Quaker healer, has worked with people with AIDS, veterans, tortured refugees, sexual abuse survivors, inmates, and ritual abuse survivors. The American Friends Service Committee, a Quaker organization, has advocated for LGBTQ+ rights since the 1960s.

42. Mary E. Banghart Therrien, "Don't take away our teacher," *Between the Lines*, January 1996, p. 10.

43. Annie Laurie Gaylor, "Listening In On the Christian Coalition 'Road to Victory' 1995," Freedom From Religion Foundation, October 1995. https://ffrf.org/component/k2/item/18522-listening-in-on-the-christian-coalition-road-to-victory-1995

44. See Note 22.

45. David Zeitler, letter to superintendent, December 4, 1995.

46. Theodore H. MacDonald, letter to school board and superintendent, December 4, 1995.

47. Marilyn Gritter, letter to school board, December 12, 1995.

48. Gary Carpenter, Fay Carpenter, letter to school board, December 12, 1995.

49. Gary Rillema, Melissa Heckard, letter to school board's personnel committee, November 26, 1995.

50. Gary Rillema, Melissa Heckard, letter to school board's personnel committee, November 26, 1995.

51. *The Grand Rapids Press*, Wyoming/Byron Center Edition, December 7, 1995. p. 3.

52. Mike Stephens, "Byron Center: A Study in Abuse," *Advocate*, Kent County's Michigan Education Association newsletter, March 1996.

53. The process of coming out begins internally. The length of time between coming out to oneself and to another person can be as long as months, years, or decades.

54. Oxford dictionary – espouse - to give your support to a belief, policy, etc.

55. Kathleen Hart, letter to school board president Robert Kaiser, December 31, 1995.

56. According to the *Pickering-Connick test*, based on two US Supreme Court cases, *Pickering v. Board of Education,* 391 U.S. 563 (1968) and *Connick v. Myers*, 461 U.S. 138 (1983), the initial question is whether the public employee spoke on a matter of public concern, defined as a matter of larger societal significance or importance, as opposed to a personal, private matter. If it was a matter of public concern, then the court must balance the employee's right to free speech against the employer's interests in an efficient, disruptive-free workplace.

   In 2006, the US Supreme Court imposed another obstacle for public employees seeking to protect their free speech rights. Public employees must also prove that they spoke as citizens, not pursuant to their official job duties. *Garcetti v. Ceballos*, 547 U.S. 410 (2006).

57. Douglas A. Nave, "The Debate over Ordained Service by

Homosexual Persons in the Presbyterian Church (U.S.A.)," *Journal of Lutheran Ethics*, January 1, 2003.

58. Alan Keyes lost his presidential election in 1996. In 2004 Keyes unsuccessfully ran against Barack Obama for US Senator of Illinois.

59. *Gay Rights, Special Rights* was produced by Jeremiah Films and can be viewed here. https://www.youtube.com/watch?v=XTvqla_YK5I&list=PL71E90B032BE37F37

60. David Prindle, letter to the editor, *The Grand Rapids Press*, Wyoming/Byron Center Edition, March 19, 1996 .

61. ACT-UP, the AIDS Coalition to Unleash Power, was born of anger—AIDS was a public health crisis being treated by the Reagan Administration and the states as a gay disease of little import. The organization's motto, "Silence = Death," highlighted the problem.

62. Formerly, GLSTN, the Gay and Lesbian Independent School Teacher Network.

63. The signatories of the "Open Letter to the Community of Byron Center," which urged people "to vote for candidates who unashamedly espouse the moral standards that made our nation great" included Rev. Richard Gregory of Byron Center Bible Church, Rev. Thomas C. Vanden Heuvel of First Byron CRC, Rev. John Gorter of Byron Center Second Byron CRC, Rev. Duane Vander Klok of (now known as) Resurrection Life Church, Grandville, Rev. Dale R. Cross of Abundant Life Church, and Rev. Etheridge H. Moore of Heritage Baptist Church. In 2012, Rev. Moore was convicted of embezzling of over $100,000 from his church.

64. Jill Smolowe, "The Unmarrying Kind," *Time*, April 29, 1996, p. 68.

65. In August 1995 the Merrimack School Board adopted policy 6540, "Prohibition of Alternative Lifestyle Instruction," which prohibited the "encouraging or supporting of homosexuality as a positive lifestyle alternative." A Walt Whitman video and Shakespeare's play "Twelfth Night" were removed from their English courses. The New Hampshire ACLU, National ACLU, Gay & Lesbian Advocates and Defenders (GLAD), and People for the American Way filed and supported a lawsuit against the school district based on the First Amendment. As a

result of the lawsuit and a school board election, the district repealed the policy in May 1996.

66. See Note 64.

67. Fountain Street Church's social justice history includes hosting speakers such as Malcom X and Susan B. Anthony, whose activism in the suffrage movement was controversial at the time, and was one of first churches to perform funerals for people who died of AIDS in the 1980s.

68. The UCC uses the term "Open and Affirming" to describe churches that welcome the full participation of LGBTQ+ people in the denomination's life and ministry. Presbyterian churches use the term "More Light." In 1996, most Christian denominations considered homosexuality a sin and were not interested in affirming gay people. Since then many people have formed groups to either work for inclusion in their denomination or, where that is not possible, to provide a supporting environment for gay people who want to remain in their denomination. Examples include: Dignity USA (Catholic), Integrity (Episcopalians), Reconciling Works (Lutherans), and Room for All (Reformed Church in America).

69. See Appendix A for the list of signatories to "A Pastoral Letter from Concerned Clergy in West Michigan."

70. Charles Honey, "Ministers ask Christians to accept gays," *The Grand Rapids Press*, June 2, 1996, p. A1.

71. Honey, "Ministers ask."

72. The Michigan law "Crime Against Nature or Sodomy" states that any person "who shall commit the abominable and detestable crime against nature either with mankind or with any animal" is guilty of a felony. MCL 750.158; until *Lawrence v. Texas*, 539 U.S. 558 (2003).

73. Mary Banghart Therrien, "Don't take away our teacher," *Between the Lines*, January 1996, p. 10.

74. The English poet Christina G. Rossetti wrote the poem, "In the Bleak Midwinter."

75. Mary Banghart Therrien, *Between the Lines*, January 1997.

76. Cardiomyopathy is defined at https://www.mayoclinic.org/

diseases-conditions/cardiomyopathy/symptoms-causes/syc-20370709
and idiopathic is defined at https://www.webmd.com/heart-disease/
heart-failure/qa/what-is-the-definition-of-idiopathic.

77. In the film, Richard Dreyfuss plays Mr. Holland, a high school music teacher whose love of music and talent for teaching motivates and inspires his students.

78. "Discouraging signs," *The Grand Rapids Press*, April 22, 1997.

79. Having lost its "appeal of right" to the Michigan Court of Appeals, the school's remaining option would have been to seek a discretionary appeal, referred to as an Application for Leave to Appeal, to the Michigan Supreme Court. In a discretionary appeal, the court makes an initial decision about whether it is willing to even accept the appeal. Less than five percent of these applications are granted.

80. The Freedom of Information Act (FOIA) is a law which provides a mechanism for people to obtain copies of government documents. An essential part of our democracy, the law requires government officials to promptly provide the documents requested, or provide a legally justified reason why it will not or cannot do so.

81. Ted Roelofs, "Cost of Crane dispute remains a mystery," *The Grand Rapids Press*, September 15, 2000, p. C1.

82. This is based on the amount the school reported paying, $17,000 between March 1999 to mid-2000, plus estimates of interest, costs, and consideration of the type of fees it would have incurred between the end of December 1996 to March 1999.

83. Theresa D. McClellan, "We should not be seen as separate worlds," *The Grand Rapids Press*, April 30, 1997, p. B1.

84. The Gay, Lesbian, Straight Education Network (GLSEN) is a national organization that serves the needs of LGBTQ+ youth. The organization was founded by Kevin Jennings, a former teacher. Jennings served as Assistant Deputy Secretary for the Office of Safe and Drug-Free Schools in the US Department of Education during 2009–2011. He currently serves as the CEO of Lambda Legal.

85. Aaron Cassette helped form this GLSEN chapter.

86. Ben Boerkoel, Pam McComb, Colleen Cusick, Dave Watt, Joanne

Simmons, and Phyllis Baker served on the chapter's first board of directors.

87. The Freedom of Association clause of the First Amendment protects the right of public school students to form clubs. A school could, however, prevent the formation of a specific club, like a GSA, by prohibiting all clubs. Contact GLSEN, the ACLU, or Lambda Legal if your school opposes your efforts to start a GSA. See the federal Equal Access Act and the ACLU's website for legal information about starting a GSA. https://www.aclu.org/other/how-start-gay-straight-alliance-gsa.

88. See Ari Beser, "How Paper Cranes Became a Symbol of Healing in Japan," National Geographic Society Newsroom, August 23, 2015, https://blog.nationalgeographic.org/2015/08/28/how-paper-cranes-became-a-symbol-of-healing-in-japan.

89. GIFT's website is https://www.giftgr.org.

90. The Grand Rapids Windfire chapter, a group for LGBTG+ youth, was started in 1984 by Michael May. Given the dearth of youth groups in the 1980s, teenagers would come from as far as Traverse City, 140 miles away, to attend a meeting. Kym Duursma led the group for twelve years until it disbanded in 2004.

91. Fred Sebulske, as founder and director of Actors' Theatre from 1981 to 2010, has brought innovative works to Grand Rapids, including those with LGBTQ+ themes. He directed *Corpus Christi* by Terrence McNally and *March of the Falsettos* by William Finn, and he presented *The Normal Heart* by Larry Kramer and the world premiere of *Seven Passages: The Stories of Gay Christians* by Stephanie Sandberg.

92. Quote is from promotional material for the play.

93. *The Grand Rapids Press*, April 30, 1997.

94. During the fundraisers, Margarethe Cammermeyer told her story including her legal battle to get reinstated into the military. Lambda Legal had filed a lawsuit on her behalf and she was eventually reinstated. Her 1994 autobiography, *Serving in Silence*, was made into a movie the following year.

Index

CPSIA information can be obtained
at www.ICGtesting.com
Printed in the USA
LVHW102303100522
718468LV00004B/291